Landmark
BOOKS

# CHIEF OF THE COSSACKS

# CHIEF OF THE
# COSSACKS

**HAROLD LAMB**

Illustrated by Robert Frankenberg

RANDOM HOUSE · NEW YORK

# CONTENTS

*On the other side of the earth there is a mighty river called the Volga. Its name means the Great Water.*

*Like our Father of Waters, the Mississippi, for a long time the Volga was a frontier. Once the Mongols of Genghis Khan grazed their herds along its banks. They were called the Golden Horde because their Khan dwelt in pavilions of cloth-of-gold. After the Golden Horde lost its power, the men of Muscovy— from the city of Moscow—appeared on the banks of the Volga. They were traders and settlers at first, then the soldiers who built log forts. They claimed the mighty Volga for their master, the Tsar of Muscovy.*

*At that time, more than three centuries ago, the prairies of the Volga became a vast frontier between the nomads of Asia and the town-dwelling Muscovites, or Russians. That was the day when Stenka Razin ruled the frontier of the Volga.*

*Stenka Razin was neither Tsar nor Khan. His empire was a wilderness. He dwelt not in a city but on a fleet of river boats. Some called him a pirate, and others named him the Chief of the Cossacks. But his power was greater than that of kings. There was no other man of his day quite like him.*

*His story was told not in histories but in songs that*

*you can hear today—the songs of Stenka Razin, the Chief.*

*This is the story of what he did, and how he came to be like no other man.*

# CHIEF OF THE COSSACKS

# I

# THE WILD LANDS

Stenka grew up in the vast steppes or prairies. They were called the wild lands. He never went to school, because there was no school or anyone to teach him.

But he learned the lessons of the prairies themselves. First of all, how to net fish in the river, and wild-fowl in the dense reeds of the bank. When he was given an old musket, he had to hunt out the wolves and jackals that sneaked around his home. After that he learned to ride out into the blast of the great winds, to drive home the grazing horses that might otherwise be driven to death by the terrible whirling wind.

Stenka's home, with its clay brick walls and thatched roof, stood deep in a hollow by the small river. Oak trees grew in the watered hollow and the grass remained green during the summer droughts. Also, the hollow protected his home from the whirlwinds, and from being seen by raiding Tartars. His mother and sisters took care of their cow and the few fat-tailed sheep—that was women's work. They also planted a field of barley down by the shore, to provide soup in winter.

So when he was ten years old, Stenka's work kept him out on the trackless prairie, herding the horses, hunting game, and watching for the appearance of any enemies in the high grass. For after the spring thaw, when ice flooded out of the river, the rank grass grew high as the boy's belt, and when he rode far, it was often hard to find his way home again.

"If it's light," his father told him, "your horse will spy out the track. If it's dark, he'll smell it out. But in snow or in storm, he'll depend on his master. And that's you."

Usually Stenka had no companions out on the steppe because his father and Ivan, his older brother, stayed away most of the time at the meetings or the wars over on the river Don. Sometimes when snow bound all the earth, and ice locked the waters, Stenka did not find his way home until long after starlight. Then he was glad to sight the gleam of window light down in the gully, and come through the door into the warm, whitewashed room, to take off his lambskin hat and cross himself before the bright ikon-image of St. Nicholas, the Protector of Wanderers.

His mother trusted that St. Nicholas would bring him back safely but she always wept when his father and Ivan mounted to ride off to the portage to the Don. She cared nothing that they had won honor for themselves in the wars. "Nay," she cried, weeping, "you have bled with many wounds for the honor of the great Tsar alone. And what has he ever done for the like of you?"

His father said that the Tsar sold good grain and gunpowder to his children on the river Don. But it seemed to Stenka that his father shot away 'most all the powder, and gave away the grain for brandy to get drunk on the road home. He heard that when he was born his father, Timofe, put a sword into his cradle, saying, "Cossack, this will be your companion as long as you live; this will be more than your wife. Use it well, and die with it in your hand."

Yet soon after that—so people said—his mother went alone up the river to the gorge of the rapids. Thither she fetched the old Kolduna, or Spell-woman. She put silver into the hand of the Kolduna and the old woman came to Stenka's cradle, bringing with her certain herbs, stones from a grave, and a feather from a raven. What she did with these things no one knows, but she said a spell over the child: *May thy body be like to this stone, safe from thrown missile or feathered arrow or stroke of steel.*

So after that dwellers along the river said to each other that little Stenka could never be harmed by sword, arrow or bullet. Some of them made a jest of it, and it caused both good and ill in Stenka's life.

The truth was that Stenka learned to guard his own life, like other Cossack boys, against the dangers that beset his prairies. He learned to swim the rivers in flood tide by slipping from his saddle and holding to the mane of his swimming horse. He learned to capture wild horses that roamed over the steppes by using a Tartar lasso—a noosed cord on a long, light pole. With the pole he cast the noose over the head of the swift, wild animal; then he pulled in on the cord until he could grip the mane of the horse and hold it fast.

Now such happenings on the steppes of the Cossacks were not written down in histories, or made into plays like those of Shakespeare who had not been dead long in western Europe. Instead of that, the Cossacks told about them in the settlements. Old men wandering with guitars collected these sayings into songs. That is why we read so little about Stenka Razin in the histories of Europe; his life was related in these songs of the old minstrels who often added things out of their imagination.

These minstrels made up a song of the wild prairie —the steppe itself, the wild land that had never been ploughed or harvested.

*Not with ploughs*
*But with sharp Tartar spears*
*Are our fields ploughed.*
*Not with harrows*

*But with swift horse hooves*
*Are our lands harrowed——*
*And sown with brave Cossack lives,*
*And watered with bitter tears.*

The day that Vaska Usk and his band came down the river bank they dragged along a chained black bear they had caught. The men of Vaska Usk kept their fishing boats behind the hill where the river flowed into the mighty Volga. But they used their boats to catch not fish, but goods like fine damask cloth or pearls from the merchants' barges.

When Stenka ran out to look at the captured bear, Vaska Usk hailed him merrily. The chief of the brigands had been drinking corn brandy. *"Hai!"* Come here, Cub. They say no weapon can pierce your hide. Well, then—are you afraid of the bear's teeth and claws?"

He gave Stenka a strong wooden club, and loosed the black bear's chain. With so many grown men watching, Stenka would not run away. Instead, he jumped at the bear.

He knew how bears slashed at you with their paws to knock you down and tear you. He knew that a

*He gave Stenka a club and loosed the bear's chain.*

wooden club would not hurt such an animal except on the muzzle, where the nose was tender. So he whacked the beast across the muzzle, and the bear roared, trying to seize the club in its teeth. Then it dropped to its four feet and shambled off, with Stenka unhurt.

So the men of Vaska Usk swore that Stenka could not be pierced by the claws or teeth of an animal. But it was really his skill in fighting the bear that had protected him.

# II

# FIRE ON THE STEPPE

As he grew older, the son of Timofe learned that the greatest danger on the steppe came not from blizzards or hunger but from raiders.

Somewhere, far from the frontier, families dwelt side by side in great wooden houses, with streets instead of roads running past, and armed watchmen making the rounds at night with a lantern to drive away thieves. Priests sprinkled the doors with holy water to keep out goblins and vampires.

Stenka had never seen such a town as that. Other Cossack boys who had traveled to Cherkask, the hamlet on the river Don, called him Dumb Head.

However, by taking his father's horses to graze as far as the hill of Vaska Usk, Stenka had seen a fine fleet of the Moscow merchants sailing up the Volga after the floods. Their stately vessels were larger than houses; brass cannon gleamed on the decks. Soldiers guarding them had coats of bright cloth over their shoulders. The gay sound of their flutes and singing came over the water. Stenka longed to make a journey on such great sea-going vessels, safe from grass fires and raiders alike.

Once he had to face both those dangers at once. It was near the end of the autumn drought, before the first snow. First of all, he sighted dark smoke, not drifting but swirling up from one place. Then it spread swiftly with the wind, and red gleams showed where the flames soared over tangled dry growth.

Mounting his pony, Stenka whistled to the other three horses which were moving restlessly as they scented smoke. At a trot he led them across the path of the prairie fire, but kept on watching it.

Here and there animals broke from cover to flee downwind—swift gray foxes, antelope, and a plunging, wide-horned *taur* or wild ox. Presently Stenka sighted what he had been searching for. Three riders clad in dark hides came into view, heading for the circling antelope. By the way they crouched forward, with one arm out, he knew them to be Tartars using bows. One of them had started the fire to drive game toward the others. These hunters did not care what destruction they caused if they could slay and carry off some of the fleeing animals.

To escape their notice Stenka turned his restless horses down into the gully of a stream. He and his horses could keep out of the path of the fire easily enough. Over his head giant bustards winged away from the heat; through the dry grass beneath him startled quail scuttled.

Ahead of him a half dozen fat-tailed sheep plunged clumsily along the stream. The goat that guided these sheep had gilt horns and a red cross painted on its back. The small goat had been marked in this fashion by the girl Alena from a cottage up the river. Now Alena herself ran ahead of the goat, calling to it. Her dark hair tossed in the wind and one hand gripped her skirt high as she ran, panting.

Reining in his pony, Stenka kept behind the fleeing sheep with his horses. He was angry at the senseless girl for wandering so far with stupid sheep. After sighting him, dark Alena tossed her head and tried to make her goat go faster. The goat, however, wanted to stop to drink from the stream.

After a while Stenka turned his mount up the side of the gully to observe the fire. It was passing harmlessly beyond the gully. But the three Tartar hunters were coming swiftly up the stream behind him. They must have sighted the track of his horses or the fleeing girl.

Now Stenka realized that the fast Tartar *Kabarda* horses could overtake his herd, if he tried to flee. And they would certainly take the sheep from the frightened girl.

Deciding quickly to face them at the stream, Stenka went back to it and slid from his saddle, looking to the priming of his short firelock gun. Instead of praying to St. Nicholas he dropped three more bullets into the barrel.

The Tartar riders plunged through the brush and halted at sight of the Cossack boy with a raised gun. They held their short bows strung, and their broad faces shone with sweat.

"Out of my way!" shouted Stenka. Because his mother was a Tartar by birth, he was familiar with the language and could speak to the raiders.

"*Ai-a, batcha!*" one of them responded. "Hi, boy! Mount and ride away from the fire!"

Then Stenka knew they were trying to trick him, because if he mounted his pony he could not aim his clumsy firelock, while the wily Tartars could handle their short bows well enough from the saddle. They crouched lower, close to the necks of their horses, their tempers inflamed by the hunt.

Anger swept through Stenka like a hot wave. He fired his gun at the middle man, and some of the bullets hit, because the warrior grunted and his horse swerved into the one near it. Again Stenka pointed his gun, as if it had another barrel ready to fire. The Tartars turned and fled, two of them guiding the injured man.

All this time the girl Alena had watched anxiously from boulders by the stream. When Stenka had loaded

*He rode out to the tracks left by the raiders and*

his firelock carefully and mounted his pony to make
certain the raiders had gone off and not circled back to
slay him, she offered him the barley cakes and dried
raisins she had tied up in her kerchief. She touched the
silver image of St. Nicholas hanging at her slender

*followed them to the tent-village of the Tartar hunters.*

throat, and hastily bound up her loose hair into her head kerchief so that she would be modestly covered before the young warrior.

"Cossack," she exclaimed cheerfully, "I prayed to Saint Nicholas, and your bullet went true to your aim."

Wetting the dry raisins in the stream and gulping them down—for he was thirsty by then—Stenka did not tell her that he had slipped not one but four bullets into his gun. And because she had greeted him as a grown Cossack, not as a boy, he did not scold her for straying too far with her pet goat and sheep.

But the next day when the wind ceased, he took care to ride out to the tracks left by the raiders and follow them to the *aul*, or tent-village, of the Tartar hunters. At a foot pace he rode among the tents. Then, dismounting by the hearth fire of the aul, he found the wounded man waiting among the others who watched him silently.

Gravely then Stenka told them how he sought peace; how he and the Tartar warrior should pour water on their swords. By that he meant they would have no blood feud between them. He did not want to be hunted down by the skilled Tartar horsemen, and he offered the injured man a slain antelope as a gift.

When the Tartar touched the gift of the dead animal, Stenka took his departure without more misgivings. The Tartars would not attack him after he had passed beyond the line of their tents, which was the limit of their hospitality.

After that it was said on the steppe that Stenka had become blood-brother to the tribal folk. Alena sometimes waited with her sheep for him to drive in the small horse herd at evening.

"Is it true, son of Timofe," she asked, "that the spell laid upon you wards off bullets and arrows?"

Stenka laughed because she seemed anxious. "Eh, lass, I do not intend to make a test of it. The Tartars say that for every man there is a bullet marked. Who knows the truth?"

III

# KHAN OF THE KALMUKS

Another thing made people talk about the young son of Timofe. He often went alone across the wide Volga and came back unhurt.

Up in the north when the spring floods came, mighty Mother Volga swept through dark forests and roared between white chalk cliffs. In the southern prairies, however, the great river merely spread over the plain until at times you could not see where the water ended and the land began. Even the men of Vaska Usk seldom ventured across the river.

The steppes over there were marked by *kurgans*— great mounds of earth where people had been buried in ancient times. Wanderers who passed these kurgans at night believed that the dead souls whispered and called to them from the mounds. Stenka himself thought he heard them breathing under the earth when the moon was bright. But he might have heard the wind rustling the tall dry grass.

Then, too, the Black Kalmuks lived in these steppes. The Black Kalmuks had yellowish faces and slant eyes; they clad themselves in dark wolfskins. Not long before, they had come out of far Asia to escape from the power of the Emperor of Cathay. They brought along small temples, with strange gods, mounted on wagon wheels. It was said that these Kalmuks carried off Christian children for slaves. But they never laid hand on Stenka who had grown almost as tall as a man.

He used to cross the Volga with his pony in a barge, poling over the shallows and then drifting across the current with the wind. He liked to watch the Kalmuk horsemen hunting down herds of wild horses in the early spring, when the wild animals were too weak and thin to run fast. Since Stenka's pony could not keep up with the swift pacer horses of the pagan warriors, he would watch the chase from a height. The Kalmuks used lassos of noosed hide ropes fastened to the ends of long poles. When they halted to eat at the end of a hunt, they gave the boy a bowl of milk curds and barley water. In this way after a time Stenka learned that, whatever the fierce Kalmuks might do on a raid, they would not attack a visitor in their own grazing lands.

Once when the ice was gone from the Volga and the yellow crocuses flamed across the prairie, some elders from the Council of the Don Cossacks rode by Stenka's home. These proud old warriors came that way because Ivan Razin guided them.

The Councilors were trying to find the Kalmuk Khan and they were looking for barges to cross the Volga with their horses. They wore gold-plated belts, and their red boots had silver heels. As it happened Stenka could tell them where to look for the pagan Khan. He was with the camp of the wild-horse hunters.

The men from the Don looked at Stenka attentively.

"How do you know it is the Khan?" they asked him.

Carefully Stenka explained. "Because the Khan sits to watch on a white horsehide; because the standard pole in front of his tent has nine horsetails."

"Eh, Cub," they said then, "show us the way to him."

Ivan, his brother, was very pleased when Stenka led the elder men of the Don over the river, past the mounds of the kurgans toward the white gleam of a salt desert where the Kalmuks had their camp. No sooner had the Cossacks come in sight of it than a band of Kalmuk bowmen circled down toward them warily, trying to discover if they had come in war or peace. Then the Cossack elders raised their arms, holding up fine muskets, shirts of chain mail and silver goblets— the gifts they brought to the Kalmuk Khan. After that they were allowed to enter the camp.

Stenka did not understand very well why these men had sought the pagan Khan. Perhaps it was to swear a firm friendship, so there would be neither raiding nor war between the Cossack brotherhoods and the Kalmuk horde.

But when they left, the white-bearded Khan gave them presents of sable skins and carved jade of Cathay.

*The Cossacks brought gifts to the Kalmuk Khan.*

He even gave a young horse to Stenka. This was a black Kabarda, trained to the saddle; it ran with its head held high to watch over the tall grass, and it did not gallop headlong but went with a swaying pace that never tired Stenka. He could let the Kabarda graze loose, without a picket line, because the swift black horse would come in from beyond his sight at his whistle.

One of the elder Cossacks offered Stenka a heavy handful of silver coins of Muscovy for this young horse. But Stenka would not sell him, and Ivan, who knew the rights of such a matter, said that the boy should not part with the Kabarda because it was a gift from the powerful Khan.

It was because of the Kabarda that Stenka Razin won his first fame in the wars.

## IV

# THE CANNON AT AZOV

All that year of 1641 the armed host of the Don Cossacks had been besieged by the Turks at the fort of Azov. Riders went from hamlet to hamlet in the steppes, begging for gunpowder and grain to be sent to the besieged Cossacks.

Now when any Cossacks were in danger, like this, the others tried to help. They had to manage for themselves because they had no king, or parliament, or army of the ordinary kind. They were simply the free frontiersmen of the prairies beyond the reach of any government.

When the Golden Horde ruled the steppes, the arrogant Tartars spoke of these white hunters as *Kazaks,* or Wanderers, and they kept the name for themselves. So fiercely independent were they that they acknowledged no master. When they wanted to decide a matter, the grown-up fighting men of a country would gather in a *Rada,* or Circle—what we call a Council— and if there was any fighting to be done, which usually happened, they chose one of their elders to be *Ataman* —Father-Commander.

Since they had had to fight to keep alive for two centuries, these free Cossacks had come to dwell along the great rivers that flowed through their prairies to the inland seas. For protection they built their encampments sometimes on islands and sometimes where streams flowed into the great rivers. Since the Cossacks made their own longboats, they were able to take to the boats to journey up and down the wide waterways, where mounted Tartars or Turks or even the trained armies of the Polish King could not get at them. Then, too, the Cossacks often sailed in their small fleets to raid other lands, or pillaged the convoys of merchants coming up the rivers. They were so daring and crafty at this that they were feared by others in spite of their small numbers. They had a saying, "Only victorious Cossacks return alive to the camps."

As time went on, many refugees came from the northern towns to the open prairies—outlaws escaping arrest, hunters seeking wild game, or starving peasants looking for free land. The Cossacks called these refugees the *Golytba*, the Homeless; they were safe enough, if they could manage to live on the prairies, because the Cossacks would not give up people who took refuge among them.

Since these free Cossacks lived along the rivers, they formed first the Host of the river Dnieper, and then, farther to the east, the Host of the Don, which flowed quietly down to the Black Sea. The Volga, being farthest to the east, had no such Host as yet among the pagan Kalmuks and Nogai Tartars. But when the appeal for food and powder came from the Cossacks besieged by the Turks on the Don, those on the Volga did what they could to answer it. Stenka Razin was glad to go with his Kabarda pacer, taking saddle bags of barley, because he knew his brother was shut up with the others on the Don.

Swiftly he rode along the portage between the two rivers. More and more riders joined him, some leading laden packhorses. When they reached the bank of the gray Don, warriors were waiting with a flat barge to float the sacks of food and powder down the river to the fort. Because he wanted to join his brother, Stenka went on the massive barge, taking his black horse with him, although he was still too young to serve in a Cossack regiment.

It was no easy matter to reach the besieged fort, because the great army of the Turkish Sultan was in camp around it. The Cossack warriors floated the barge through the Turkish lines at night in a mist, and kept off a patrol boat by firing a few shots. They heard the dull boom of cannon downstream a long time before they poled in safely behind the earthworks that defended the Cossack fort on the shore.

When daylight came through the mist, Stenka saw that the weary Cossacks in the fort were thin with hunger. They snatched at wheat from the barge and rubbed it in their fists to make it easier to chew. Before any of the food could be cooked the Ataman of the Don appeared in the courtyard with his colonels behind him. This commander carried an ivory baton and had a white fur kaftan thrown over his shoulders. All the men who were not at the cannon or on watch gathered around him in a circle and when the stern Ataman began to speak, all took off their black lambskin hats.

"Brothers," said the Ataman for all to hear, "I have a message from the Pashas who command our enemies. Hear it and tell me how you, Cossack brothers, will answer it."

Then the scribe who accompanied the Ataman read from a paper how the Sultan of the Turks would pardon the Cossack brigands and robbers who had seized his fort. They could go free and carry out their weapons and silver—if they would leave the fort to his army. He warned them not to hope for aid from the Christian Tsar of Moscow, who cared nothing for such thieves as they.

Immediately the listening warriors began to laugh. They would not think of such surrender. Some of them cried out that they had aid already from their brothers on the Dnieper and the Volga.

"Tell those Turks, those slaves of the Sultan, to march away to their ships," shouted one of the Don men. "Or they will leave their Turkish bodies here on the Don to be food for our gray eagles and black ravens."

The Ataman listened to all of them and agreed. "I will say that we will never leave this fort until it pleases us to do so. Ay, and then we will sail to the city of the Sultan and look at it, and if it pleases us, we will take it for our own and keep his Pashas to serve as our swineherds."

So did the hard-pressed garrison of Azov defy the demand of the Turks to surrender. But Ivan Razin was not pleased to find his younger brother Stenka within the ramparts of the fort. "The chances are you will not get out with a whole hide," he grumbled. "And they'll kill that black nag of yours for meat."

At the thought of the wise, knowing Kabarda being killed, Stenka's temper flamed. Usually he was silent and quiet but when blind rage seized him he would listen to nobody. Moreover, by now he was as tall and as powerful in build as his brother Ivan, the soldier.

"Whatever you say, Stenka," Ivan grunted, "your horse won't live long. There's nothing to feed him here."

Whereupon Ivan went away to his duty, and all that day Stenka watched over the black Kabarda, which was tied in an empty shed. He noticed how the Cossack cannon began to fire back in answer to the bombardment of the Turks. Because they had more powder now in the fort. After dark he led his horse quietly down to the river. The Kabarda pushed eagerly toward the grass along the bank. Neither Stenka nor his pony had had anything to eat for a night and a day. Watching out carefully for Turkish sentries, the boy led his treasured pony farther out over the plain to graze.

Then he noticed a strange thing. The booming of the Turkish guns dwindled away and changed to the rumbling of distant wagons. Although watchfires flamed in the enemy's lines, he could see no men moving around them.

After an hour's stealthy search, Stenka understood that the Turkish soldiers were retreating from their siege works. At once he mounted the grazing horse and rode back to the ramparts of the Cossacks. When the sentries heard his message, they called an officer who hurried the boy to the hut of the Ataman. The old commander peered at the boy with the hooded eyes of an eagle. "Speak up, Cub. Why do you believe they are going away, like wolves leaving their prey?"

Holding his hat in his tense hands as he had seen the others do, the young Stenka explained. "Because, Father, their standard poles no longer showed against the sky—because the sound of their wagons went away toward the sea."

At this the Ataman lifted his gray head with pride. "Glory to God! Then the pagan host may sail away." He looked quickly at the anxious boy. "Can you follow them, Cub, and watch?"

"Ay. If you, Father, will give command not to slay my horse for meat."

The listening Cossack officers laughed at the boy, but the Ataman did not. "I command it, Stenka Razin."

So it happened that Stenka was one of the first to see—when the dawn mist cleared—that the Turkish army was embarking on its galleys drawn up on the white salt shore. Some of the weary Cossacks believed that their answer to the demand of the Sultan's Pashas had discouraged the Turks; others thought that the

*Stenka rode back to the ramparts of the Cossacks.*

fresh supply of powder had saved them. But the real reason for raising the siege was that the resistance of the Cossacks had cost the Turks too many lives.

Stenka became a *kunak*, or brother of the Don Cossacks. They no longer called him *ouchar*—a young cub. With a warrior's sword and lance he could take his place in their host.

"There is a devil in you, Stenka," his brother told

him. "You follow your own path in danger, yet no harm comes to you."

Still, the Cossacks could not keep their fort at Azov. The ambassadors of the dreaded Sultan complained angrily to the far-off Tsar in Moscow, and the Tsar bade the Host of the Don give up the fort they had seized at the river mouth. They did not want to do it, after so many had died to defend it. But they could not stand against the power of the Sultan and the Tsar as well.

When they left Azov, they hauled away all their cannon and burned all their buildings, so that nothing remained except the empty ramparts.

Stenka never forgot how the labor of the Cossacks had gone for nothing at the will of the strange Tsar.

V

# BELLS OF MOSCOW

Stenka Razin was many years older when he saw the face of this Tsar of Muscovy. By then he had grown to his full strength; he could lift a powder keg with each outstretched arm. Because he labored willingly he was given hard tasks to do. Yet no one had taught him to read any lettering. He was called *Durak*—Dumb Head

—because he understood only how to track down animals or build longboats to explore the rivers. At that kind of thing, no one was as quick as the giant son of Timofe.

He rode all the way to Moscow of the White Wall because he had been ordered to guide a detachment of twenty Cossacks thither to enter the service of the Tsar. It was early spring of 1662, with old snow still beneath the pine coverts and mud deep in the road. But within the guarded gate of the White Wall of Moscow, logs had been laid in the streets to keep people from slipping into the mud. The Cossacks from the steppe had made the long journey easily enough, but they did not know where to turn or what to do in this vast city of the Muscovites.

For it seemed to be several towns, one town crowded within another—first within the gray Earth Wall, then within the stone White Wall, after that the China-town of the merchants of Cathay, and finally the Red Town all of brick around the towers of the Kremlin. Beside the Kremlin stretched the Red Place where guards waited in pairs. Unlike the Cossacks these guards wore green-and-red uniforms and they carried fine muskets. The ordinary Muscovites who crowded around a great wooden platform wore long coats that stretched to the muddy ground, and they kept talking in whispers about a new kind of money. The Cossacks asked if someone would be hanged on the platform, because it was called the Place of Execution.

The Muscovites said no, that the Tsar himself was coming to his palace within the Kremlin. It seemed strange to Stenka Razin that a gibbet stood here at the gate of the palace.

Then the Tsar came riding on a white, ambling horse, with palace guards walking before and behind and on each side. These tall men, splendid in ermine kaftans, carried long silver axes to keep back the pressing throng. Some of the people fell on their knees as the Tsar passed, but others struggled toward him to catch hold of his stirrups and the skirts of his cloth-of-gold coat. Tsar Alexis had a round, pleasant face under a cap shining with jewels and bordered with fur. Willingly he listened to the beseeching common people, forbidding his ax-men to strike them. He seemed to take pity on them because he struck hands with one of the mob as a token of agreement. Whereupon the crowd shouted joyfully, "He swears—the copper coins are like to silver and no less!"

It turned out that new copper kopeks had been given out by the treasurers of the Tsar in exchange for the old silver coins, and the people were afraid of being cheated. Stenka discovered this for himself that night when he tried to find a tavern to shelter himself and his horse.

Along the Volga he could find a shed for the horse and a bite and sup for himself, as well as straw to sleep on. Here in the Muscovite city muttering peasants crowded the benches. There was no bread to munch and no hay on the floor. The silent tavern keeper watched over his kegs with a cudgel in his belt. When Stenka held out a kopek and a mug to fill, the man only looked at him and spat.

"What's biting you?" Stenka demanded. The kopek had the Tsar's head stamped on it, and the Cossack himself had heard how it was worth silver. Silver for one swallow of vodka!

Stenka was growing angry, and the tavern keeper pulled out his cudgel, when a slim brown fellow hugging a gypsy's shawl pressed against Stenka's arm. "Spies in the roost," he whispered, jerking his head at the dim benches. "Don't kindle up here."

This young gypsy, who named himself Filka, had

an odd way of talking. He explained, once they were outside the tavern, how the Tsar might think the copper kopeks to be good, but the money-makers stamped copper of their own just like coins, and so most of the new kopeks were good for nothing—except to build fine palaces for the treasurers. "Come with me, Cossack," whispered the sly Filka, "and you can fill your big hide with honey-mead. Honest folk are on the way to break into the dwellings of the dogs of boyars, the treasurers." He winked up at Stenka. *"Sarin na kitchkou!* Kindle up and slay!"

While he spoke, Stenka, who always kept watch around him, noticed two dim figures come out of the tavern after them. Filka led him down the logs of the alley to the open space in front of a church tower. Here a lantern flickered on the ground. Beside it rested a woman's head projecting from the earth.

Surprised, Stenka strode over to the head. It was alive, because its eyes glared up at him and its mouth moaned. Filka, however, pulled at his arm, saying that this was merely a condemned woman or witch. She had been buried alive to die slowly.

When he heard that, Stenka became hot with rage.

The woman's eyes fastened on him. Without a word he searched until he found a digging spade by the church steps. Then he went to work swiftly to spade up the earth around her shoulders and body.

She stopped moaning and gasped hopefully. Then she cried out. Two men in gray cloaks and black hoods stepped silently into the lantern-light. So clad, they could hardly be seen at night, and Stenka judged them to be spies. One drew out a pistol, while the other took a chain from his belt. Filka had vanished from sight.

"For aiding one condemned," exclaimed the man with the weapon, "you are under arrest."

Without answering, Stenka gripped the woman's arms and pulled her out of the loosened earth. She stumbled away into the darkness, and the spy with the chain moved after her silently.

Suddenly the big Cossack swung his spade, full of dirt, into the face of the man with the pistol. Stenka was afire with rage, and he whirled the heavy spade, slashing open the head of the other man. Then the armed spy ran away, rubbing at his eyes. Filka appeared out of nowhere and pulled at the arm of the snarling Cossack.

"Fool!" whispered Filka. "Those gray weasels were following me. Now you've whacked the life out of one. Better if you'd done for both."

The sly Filka warned Stenka Razin that he must flee from Moscow's walls in the darkness or he would be tracked down. Filka wanted to take the road to the steppes to escape. But the Cossack was too angered to listen. Seeking out his horse, he mounted it. This was a roan stallion, strong enough to carry his weight swiftly. He had left the small Kabarda to graze at his home.

When rage seized him like this he always mounted to the saddle and rode out over the prairie until his blood cooled. Now he headed for an open gate of the city.

The guards at the gate paid no attention to him because the bells of all the church towers were clashing and chiming. Far behind him, near the Red Place, flames glowed in the night.

Crowds of people who had been cheated by the false copper money had broken into the house of the chief treasurer, as Filka had said, to snatch up spoil. As they did that, the great wooden palace caught fire.

The big Cossack swung his spade into the man's face.

Afterward, it was said that Stenka Razin of the Volga had led this rioting. But that was not the truth. When the officials of Moscow marked his name down for arrest and trial, he could not be found.

## VI

# THE BRANDING OF
# STENKA RAZIN

In fact, for almost a year Stenka was well hidden. The Cossacks had a saying, "When you have taken life it is good to go away to pray for your soul." And the troubled warrior from the Volga tried to do that.

For weeks he rode north, like a gray wolf slipping along the narrow tracks in the dense pine forests, until he came to the shore of the silent White Sea. There he left his horse and embarked on a fishing boat that sailed for twelve hours over tideless water before it brought him to a rocky island. On this island rose the high stone walls of the monastery of the monks of Solovetsky.

When Stenka told them he was a Cossack who wanted to pray, the monks took him inside their walls. They gave him a pallet bed in the hall where pilgrims stayed. A fat jolly monk named Chvedor took especial care of Stenka. But Chvedor could not teach the young wanderer to read, because he did not know how himself. In fact these monks of the far island did not even remember the words of the prayers too well.

It was a strange place, where the light did not leave the sky at night—since it was so near to the Arctic where the faint sun scarcely left the sky during summer. The waves beat like drums against the wall under Stenka's sleeping place, and wild sea birds swarmed around the ramparts. When the great bell of Solovetsky chimed at dusk, all the people took lighted candles and went to sing hymns in the small church where the pictures of the saints gleamed in silver frames.

For these monks of Solovetsky were old-fashioned people. They sang the old hymns, thought that Saint

Nicholas and Saint Andrew actually came down to visit human beings on the earth, and that during the hours of real darkness the Devil walked in the forest trying to snatch the souls of men. Stenka understood all this well enough, because his Tartar mother had told him the same thing. And he liked to hear the deep chant of the bearded monks, even if they did not have fiddles or bagpipes to liven up the music.

Chvedor of the fat body found wine to make them merry often enough. Chvedor said that good Saint Nicholas wanted to help wanderers on their way, and that good wine helped them, too. Stenka might have lived on well enough in this remote monastery but it seemed to him like a huge fort, where the garrison did nothing but keep themselves safe.

He grew weary of the cold island and wanted to smell the sun-warmed grass of the steppes again. Chvedor begged him to stay, because Stenka told him such merry tales of the far-off Mother Volga. But when Stenka felt the long trails calling him nothing could hold him back.

So he returned to the White Sea village and searched for his horse. The *Streltsi*, the Muscovite guards, were keeping the stallion for him at the village post-station.

When Stenka claimed it they arrested him. The judge of the court at the town of Michael Archangel sentenced him to a labor prison for murder.

What happened next we do not know very well. Such things were rarely written down in books at the time. Among the Cossacks the elder men and the wandering minstrels who played the bandura kept such events in their memories. And the Cossacks say that Stenka labored for four years in a forest prison. There the guards branded him with a hot iron on the right side of his chest, with the letters C A I N.

Many of the prisoners in that snowbound labor camp became afraid for their lives. Stenka was the only Cossack among them and he felt no fear. The guards lashed his body with steel-tipped whips until the scars were like cords in his skin. His body became strong as a bear's, and his anger grew until he could think of nothing else.

Somehow the giant Cossack managed to escape from the guarded camp. He made his way afoot over the snow trail to Archangel. In the deep darkness of a winter night, he appeared at the stables of the governor's house. There he asked the drowsy guards for his horse that had been taken away from him. You see, Stenka did not understand Muscovite laws very well. He could see why he had been punished for slaying a spy, but he did not see why his horse should have been taken away from him.

Since he wore only patched, ragged wolfskins, the Streltsi thought him to be a wandering Golytba, or homeless man. They asked his name.

Whereupon Stenka Razin pulled back his coat and shirt to show the letters branded on his chest— C A I N. "That is my name, dogs," he snarled. "And I bear it for good reason."

Seizing one of their spears, he broke it between his hands and used one end as a club, the other as a long dagger. Snatching up the whale-oil lantern, he hurled it into the dry hay on the stable floor. "*Sarin na kitch-kou!*" he roared, remembering the cry of the vagabond Filka. "Kindle up and slay!"

After flames spread through the barn, the serfs awakened by the fighting let loose the horses from their stalls. Stenka caught one of the best of the startled animals by the mane and leaped to its back. He could ride bareback, with the loose tether cord for a rein.

Swiftly he fled south. By using the broken spear point as a weapon, he took a good pair of soft leather boots

*The Cossacks say that Stenka labored for four years*

*in a forest prison. But he felt no fear.*

and a fur kaftan from other wayfarers on the road. Then he seized a saber and food for his saddle bags, saying that the wealthy Muscovites should share their things with a homeless one.

So he was well clad again when he went to seek his brother Ivan. These Cossacks all had names taken from the Bible. Stenka's brother's name was John in their speech, as Stenka was Stephen, or rather Little Steve. They called him that in jest because he was so big.

Now Stenka wanted to find his brother to ask what he should do in his trouble. For months he sought along the post roads for news of his brother, and he was glad when he heard that Ivan had been made a colonel of the Cossacks. Then he met with two of them riding south without an officer.

From these Don Cossacks Stenka heard the terrible news of his brother's death. Often enough Cossacks died in battle—that had happened to Timofe (Timothy), his father. But Ivan, who had served the great Tsar of his own free will, had been hanged like a robber.

That happened when Colonel Ivan Razin and his regiment of the Don men became ill and weary in the long winter encampment in the cold north. There was no war during the winter, and they wanted to ride south to their steppes until the Tsar might have real need of them.

But Prince Dolgoruki, the commander of the Muscovite army in Poland, forbade Ivan to go, saying that he must learn to be a soldier and obey orders instead of stealing off like a bandit. Ivan said he was a free man and that he would go when he willed. By the command of the Prince he was arrested and hanged, with the Muscovite army and its foreign officers mustered with loaded guns around the gibbet.

After that, the Don Cossacks explained, Ivan's men stole away from the army. Never again, they said, would they obey a command of the Muscovites.

Stenka Razin turned his reins, to go with them. In silence he thought about his brother's death. And he said, "I will go where the command of Prince Dolgoruki is never heard. If his governors stretch out their hands to take me, I will scorch them with fire and sword."

It seemed to be madness for one man to defy the power of the Muscovite princes. But during the long years in prison Stenka Razin had been planning how it might be done.

## VII

## TREASURE BARGES

When spring came in the year 1666, the gray ice flowed out of the rivers; the prairies turned first green and then golden and blue as flowers thrust up through the moist grass. Stenka Razin rejoiced to be in his homeland again.

He had collected only four longboats—*kaiks* that

the Cossacks rowed against the current or sailed before a breeze. About these boats some frontiersmen had gathered, eager to go after spoil with the few Don warriors who had left the Muscovite army to follow the giant Stenka because he was the brother of their slain colonel. Some of the older Don veterans wanted to sail down the river to raid the Turks who had settled in the fort of Azov and had stretched a great iron chain across the river. Stenka, however, refused to do this.

"A jackal creeps up and snatches a mouthful, fleeing when it is pursued. A wolf hunts down its prey and seizes it. Are you jackals, to snatch and run?"

They all listened to him because he spoke as an Ataman to the circle of his brothers. Usually a crowd of men who try to think what to do will follow the one who has a clear plan in his mind. Stenka intended to strengthen his band with good weapons, powder and lead for ammunition, with cattle for food, and horses to ride. And he did not intend to steal these things like a thief.

But how was he—who had neither wealth nor rank—to get such fine things without stealing them?

First, Stenka told his men, they ought to have a

standard of their own, so that people would know they were a brotherhood with a banner. For this he chose a long pole with horse-tail streamers, like his friend the Kalmuk Khan. On top of the pole he put the bleached skull of a wolf, saying that, like a wolf, he was ready to bite the wealthy Muscovites.

Next he sought the great river he knew, the Volga. He told his band that henceforth they had only their mother, the Volga, and their father, the Steppe, to aid them. Seeking out the portage he knew so well, he helped his followers tow their four longboats over the fifty-mile trail through the sagebrush. They had only a few oxen to help them in pulling one kaik after the other.

When they launched the boats in the gray flood-waters of the Volga, Stenka led his little fleet to the hill of Kamushink. This was close to his home river, the Tishina. Often from the hill he had watched the stately convoys of Tartar and Persian merchants bringing carpets and spice and silk up to the markets of Muscovy.

But now he waited patiently until long strings of barges appeared. These flew the flag of the two-headed eagle, and a cross. They carried the treasures of Muscovite princes and merchants—cloth-of-gold from India, and rich silver and jewels. Being so valuable, the barges had a multitude of Volga boatmen to tow them where the current was swift. Strong companies of Streltsi guarded them day and night.

Now Stenka's band, besides being few in number, carried poor enough weapons—except for the men of the Don who had brought along their new flintlock muskets. The others had little but clumsy matchlocks, homemade spears, and Tartar *yataghans*, or long curved knives. So Stenka chose to make his attack on the treasure barges by surprise in the darkness.

First he was careful to send messengers to the campfires of the Volga *burlaki*—the boatmen—who always spent the night on shore. His messengers warned the boatmen to stay quietly by their fires if they wanted to live.

The burlaki hesitated, unable to make out what was happening in the darkness around them. Before they could decide what to do, Stenka's band reached the barges anchored in the river.

The Cossack outlaws had tied bunches of rushes upright to the sides of their longboats. Then, lying down in the boats, they drifted down the current to the anchored vessels. In the faint starlight the drifting boats looked like small islets of reeds torn loose by the flood waters. In this manner they came unnoticed to the side of the leading vessel, which was the guard-ship with most of the soldiers.

If the Streltsi guards had been warned, the Cossacks could never have captured their bark. But most of them were asleep when Stenka climbed over the rail with his men behind him. Savagely he cut down the officers who ran out at him. The surviving soldiers fancied that the river had come alive with yelling men. *"Sarin na kitchkou!"* rang in their ears. Even their good flintlock guns could not find targets in the dark-ness. Soon only the Cossacks were alive on the guard-ship.

The soldiers posted on the anchored string of barges surrendered, because they could not join together to defend themselves.

After that night scores of the burlaki and captured soldiers joined Stenka's horse-tail standard. They were afraid of him because when daylight came they saw how each man he killed had been cut open by two strokes—one across and one down the body. They called it Stenka's cross for the souls of the dead.

*Scores joined Stenka's horse-tail standard.*

Then, too, he gave away the captured treasures with open hands. Every masterless man had a silver goblet or length of silk for his own. But most of the treasure Stenka Razin used to buy horses, ammunition and weapons. He paid for everything.

To do this he set up his standard pole in the ruined walls of Sarai on the east bank of the river. This had been the city of the Golden Horde until the Russians came and plundered it. So at first no one knew whether Tartars or Cossacks had come to dwell in haunted Sarai. Tartar merchants bound up the river began to bring their caravans over the sands to Sarai. Stenka Razin dealt with these merchants fairly. In fact he treated everyone alike, whether homeless wanderer or landowner, Christian or pagan.

One evening when he was drinking by his fire, a familiar figure slipped in. It was Filka, the gypsy, who had helped him in Moscow and who had heard of his daring deed on the Volga. When he saw the scars on Stenka's big body, Filka's thin lips twisted in a smile. "Eh, Dumb Head," he murmured, "if you'd harkened to me you'd have a whole hide now. Nay, I see well that you are still dumb as a stalled ox."

"Why a stalled ox?" demanded the giant of the Volga.

"Because you have won a small fight, you sit there scratching your hide like an ox. Truly an ox is stronger than its master, but penned in a stall it can only submit to its master. Out on the steppe it can follow its own will."

The sly Filka had a sharp tongue and no fear. Eager for more spoil, he kept at Stenka's side as his lieutenant. And between them they decided to go forth where the command of the Tsar was never heard.

## VIII

## THE HIDDEN SEA

When spring came again to the Volga in 1668, Stenka
Razin had thirty-five galleys, or larger kaiks. More
than a thousand men now followed his horse-tail standard.

As it happened, the previous year had been a hard
one. Swarms of locusts and whirling winds plagued

even the fertile steppes, while in the northern forests hunger drove people from the villages to seek bark and acorns for food. These northern people fared worse than many wild animals, so numbers of them fled to the southern prairies. More than a few sought the protection of Stenka Razin's camp.

Then, too, crowds of Old Believers began to press south. They cried out that the Devil ruled in Muscovy. And it is true that these Old Believers were persecuted by the churchmen of Moscow because they would not agree to worship in a new way. When they joined the Volga outlaws, the shrewd Filka gave them weapons.

Filka did more than that. When Stenka Razin's fleet set out down the river, it had to pass through sand bars close to the walls of Tsaritzin. This was a town at the river's edge where the famous city of Stalingrad stands today.

The prince who governed Tsaritzin ordered his cannon to fire from the walls at the galleys of the Volga men. But when matches were touched to the cannon, the guns merely smoked and flickered harmlessly with flame. No cannon shot flew out at the passing vessels.

Now everyone in Tsaritzin had heard the tale that Stenka Razin could never be harmed by bullet or steel.

They thought his magic had prevented the cannon from exploding. The governor wrote to Moscow that the pirate—as he was called—was protected from harm by magic. But the truth is that Filka had sent a few bags of silver to the cannoneers of the town, who really sympathized more with Stenka Razin than with the governor. Willingly enough these soldiers contrived matters so that their cannon did him no harm.

Past the white sand islands, past the cherry trees in bloom and the tall, waving grass, Stenka Razin sailed with his people. Beyond his homeland, his ships entered the dry sand steppe where the sky and the land seemed to stretch away to the very edge of the earth.

With him went scores of tall Cossack warriors, and short, bronzed Tartars, and keen-eyed hunters and shaggy forest men with their hand axes. To the mast of his bark was lashed the standard with the grim wolf's skull.

His men called him their Ataman of the Golytba— their Chief of the Homeless.

Down the Volga the Ataman led them, to the many mouths of the river. But where was he going? The governors of the Muscovite frontier forts asked each other that question. No one knew the answer.

Far to the east under the sun's rising lay the grazing lands of the powerful Kalmuk Khan. Far to the west, under the sun's setting, stretched the Black Sea filled with the galleys of the mighty Turkish Sultan. And, of course, far to the north ruled the Muscovite governors of the great Tsar of All the Russias.

The Ataman's people watched the reeds and sand hillocks of the Volga mouths fade into the mist behind them, and they made a song of their journey:

> *From the white island*
> *On the Mother Volga*
> *Stenka Razin's brothers*
> *Sail with a merry song.*

Ahead of them they saw a strange sea. It was a great, hidden inland sea, the Caspian. Long ago Alexander the Great had marched around it on his way to India. Its edges gleamed white with salt and sometimes orange-red with oil. No king ruled the wind-swept waves of the Caspian.

Stenka Razin determined to be its master. That first

summer he led his fleet along the shore to a smaller river in the east, the Yaik. We call it the Ural River now. Up this the Ataman sailed, to the wooden fortress of Yaisk.

This farthest frontier fort of the Muscovites had wooden towers at every corner and a gate of strong logs. Stenka Razin made no attempt to attack it.

Instead he played a trick. With two of his strongest Cossacks he put on the gray robe and hood of a pilgrim. He carried no weapon except a long pilgrim's staff. When the soldiers at the gate challenged him, asking who he might be, he shouted back that he had come to pray for them.

They did not believe that until he chanted a prayer as he had heard the monks do at Solovetsky. After that they let the three strangers in.

That night the Cossacks left their tavern and went back to the barred gate. With their staffs they beat off the guards from the gate. While the two others pulled down the bars, the Ataman climbed to the watch-tower and waved a lantern.

Then Filka and a hundred men rushed into the open gate. They had stolen up unseen in the darkness. There

*He and two of his Cossacks were garbed as pilgrims.*

was no more fighting in Yaisk. The only man of the town Stenka Razin punished was the tax collector, who had taken money from the people.

"Now we'll see," the tall Ataman said, "what good this money will do you."

The Cossacks stripped the Muscovite naked and tied a bag of gold around his neck. Then they drove him with whips out into the salt desert, where he could hardly walk barefoot among the thorns and sharp rocks.

To the fisher folk and Streltsi of the town, Stenka Razin said, "You are free now to go where you will. If you join us you will be a Cossack like me—plundering the rich boyars to give to the naked wanderers."

One hundred and sixty men joined him at Yaisk. They helped build some larger vessels of seasoned hard wood tarred along the seams. For all the Cossacks, the Volga burlaki, and the woodsmen were skilled at boat-building.

They were merry when they set out again in their strengthened fleet upon the empty waters of the Caspian. Stenka Razin told them they were going to cross the sea to the rich and fertile land of Persia where the tax gatherers of the Tsar could never reach them.

As usual, they made up new verses for their song:

> *Stenka Razin's the captain,*
> *And the Devil's the admiral——*
> *Sing a song, Princess,*
> *For we are merry today!*

IX

# COURT OF THE SHAH

Sometimes when a man shows that he will not give in to misfortune, other people come to him for help in their troubles. This happened with the Ataman, Stenka Razin.

Storm winds swept the mountainous western shore of the Caspian. The Cossack fleet was scattered by the wind and driven toward the shore. Just at that point the mountains soared to great snow peaks, the mighty Caucasus range. And the fierce people of the Caucasus feared no strangers. In fact at their port of Derbend— which means the Gate—they often seized the crews of visiting vessels to sell them as slaves to caravan merchants.

But nothing like that happened when the longboats of the Cossacks came in to the shore at Derbend. The Cossacks bunched together behind their leaders, sword and pistol in hand. They fought their way into the bazaar streets of the town, slaying and looting and burning. Most of the fierce people of Derbend were glad to take refuge in the citadel. The great stone walls of the citadel ran up the steep hill, and the Cossacks could not capture it. Still they gathered in rich spoil of damask cloth, fine ivory and shining jewels.

And even while they feasted royally at Derbend, other ships came from the Volga to join them. By then the fame of the Ataman who defied the Muscovite nobles was spreading over all the steppes and the inland seas.

From the portage, Vaska Usk brought his brigands to seek Stenka Razin on the Caspian. From the Host of the Don daring young warriors rode off to serve the new Ataman. Others came from the far River Dnieper. They were richly clad Cossacks, veterans of the wars against the Sultan—the Zaporogs, or Men from Below the Rapids. Many elders of the Cossacks shook their heads, saying that one man could not stand alone against mighty kings. Yet one of them, Krevoi, spoke up in council, declaring that this was the first time all the Cossacks had had a single Chief. Under Stenka Razin, for the first time, any Cossack or masterless man was free to live as he liked.

Seven hundred of them rallied to Krevoi. On their way down the Volga, a flotilla of boats manned with Streltsi tried to stop them. Instead of fighting them, however, most of the soldiers joined them.

So when Stenka Razin sailed from the ruins of Derbend, about five thousand men followed him in a great fleet of barks and longboats. He was taking them on to Persia itself, to settle down on new land of their own. He thought the far-off Shah of Persia would welcome these ships that were ready to serve the Shah on the Caspian. So he sent envoys ashore to ask that his Cossacks be allowed to enter Persia in peace.

Now this Shah was really a powerful emperor. His

true title was Shah-in-shah, or King-over-kings. His rule stretched from the heights of the Caucasus to the great River Indus. It seemed natural enough to him that a strange people should want to settle down under the benefit of his rule.

Yet this wealthy monarch named Suleiman lived in the luxury of garden palaces and festival halls within his beautiful city of Isfahan. He seldom went outdoors except to his throne-seat under a gilded portico where he could watch horsemen playing polo in the vast open square beneath him. Being fond of pleasure, he had only the fairest dancing girls for boon companions, and, being indolent, he let others tell him what to do.

When the strange-looking Cossack messengers arrived at the splendid court in Isfahan, they did not bring any gifts for Suleiman. They had only a small paper with Stenka Razin's request scrawled on it. No one around the Shah could read the paper, so the Cossacks had to explain what they wanted to envoys of the Tartar Khans, who in turn tried to explain it to Suleiman.

"If you come truly in peace," demanded the Persian ministers, "why do you bring cannon and powder with you and wear swords in your girdles?"

The Cossacks took off their high lambskin hats and bowed respectfully, as to an Ataman, when they answered. "We Cossacks wear sabers always to protect ourselves. Now we are willing to use our weapons in defense of the great Shah."

But the Persians, who wore jeweled turbans, did not think it a mark of respect to bare their heads and show their shaven skulls. They had never beheld Cossacks before in Isfahan, and they did not understand their customs.

The Cossack envoys were lodged splendidly in a house of blue tiles, where dainty food—spiced meats and juicy melons with cool sherbet—was brought them by the singing and dancing girls. While they feasted and waited, they thought the tree-shaded city was a place of wonder, where the people had nothing to do but amuse themselves. On the finest Arabian horses, the Cossacks showed their skill at riding before the Shah on his lofty throne, and the silk-clad throngs cried out in praise of them.

Yet the Cossacks were the guests of people strange to them. They did not understand how the Persians hid their thoughts behind smiling faces, or how the ministers around Suleiman whispered their suspicions of these unknown warriors.

For even here in lovely Isfahan, the hand of the Tsar reached out toward the Cossacks. The far-off Tsar sent an embassy of his own, with gifts of gold-plated coaches and hunting dogs, to the Shah. The Muscovites declared that the Cossacks were not a people but rebels. "They were traitors to their master Alexis, son of Michael, Tsar of Great, White, and Little Russia," argued the Muscovite envoys. "How can the Shah-in-shah, the Lord of Light, trust them within his lands?"

To this warning Suleiman and his ministers did not give much heed. The Persian monarch felt himself superior to the lord of the bare and dreary Kremlin. Besides, the Muscovites slept in their fur capes like bears, and drank all the wine within reach. They also tried to sell their sable furs for a high price secretly in the bazaar.

You see, the Persians had learned not to trust many foreigners, who seemed to want only to get their fingers into the treasures of Isfahan.

And there were other envoys, from the King of Poland and the Khan of the Krim Tartars, who whis-

*The Persian cavalry drove*

pered a different warning to the Persians. They whispered that the Cossacks came like hunting dogs, to search out land in Persia for the Tsar to seize. They merely pretended to escape from Muscovy, the envoys warned, and were really making ready to fight not for the Shah but for their old master in Moscow.

*back the stubborn Cossacks.*

Because this seemed to be such a clever trick, Suleiman Shah believed it. The Cossacks had spoken the
truth, but they could not make anyone understand that.

So it happened that the Persians refused the request
of Stenka Razin. They sent back polite words, with
costly gifts of embroidered cloth and wine of Shiraz

and wonderful silver drinking bowls. Yet the Ataman and Filka knew well enough that the Shah forbade them to stay in his country.

"We are not dogs to be driven forth," snarled Stenka Razin. And Filka said they would take what they wanted out of Persia. Whereupon they drank up all the wine out of the Shah's bowls at once, and set out to raid the countryside. It had gardens of fruit trees, caravanserais spread with rich carpets, and people clad in silk and brocade.

All this spoil the Cossacks took in their raids. Once, however, when they marched out to raid, singing their song, hosts of Persian horsemen fell upon them, riding out of the gullies into the road. The fierce Persian cavalry, clad in link mail and wielding battle-axes and light lances, drove back the stubborn Cossacks. They surrounded Stenka Razin and would have killed him if the Cossacks nearest him had not made a ring of their bodies about him.

The Cossacks were too few to stand against the disciplined army of the Shah, and they had no horses of their own. They managed to fight their way back to their ships, and to sail away. But they left many dead behind them, and many who pulled at the oars of the longboats were wounded.

Stenka Razin led them to an island near the Persian shore. On this island they could heal their wounds and be safe from the army of the Shah.

## X

# BATTLE AT SEA

As soon as Stenka Razin's followers recovered from their hurts, they wanted to sail back to the shore to avenge themselves for the defeat by the Persian horsemen. Besides, the only inhabitants of the island were humble fishermen who had neither wealth nor wine for the Cossacks.

Bands of them rowed off to raid. These fleets came back empty-handed, because wherever they drew near the fertile shore with its fine white buildings, regiments of the Shah's army rode down to meet them.

At this Stenka Razin and Filka put their heads together to think what to do. And on a day when a strong breeze blew, they selected three of the larger barks and filled them with burlaki and men of Vaska Usk who did not look at all like soldiers. Nor did Stenka Razin take any cannon on his three vessels.

Before the wind he sailed, far to the east of the Caspian to the port of Firabad. This was a town of merchants because often caravans traded there, coming from the Silk Road that led to Cathay. No Cossacks had been seen in Firabad before.

When Stenka Razin landed with his followers, they all wore the khalats or long loose coats of Oriental traders. They carried no visible weapons, having only lengths of wool cloth in their arms. But under their khalats they had hung yataghans and swords.

They pretended to be strangers in Persia who could not speak the language. Then, going into the bazaar streets, they pretended to be amazed at the fine goods of the shrewd merchants of Firabad. As if foolishly, they spent handfuls of gold ducats for trifles, and they sold the wool cloth—which they had plundered from Volga traders—at a fraction of its worth. Since they numbered only a few score, and behaved like stupid traders, the Persians thought only of getting all their money.

After the disguised Cossacks had explored the town in this fashion, they scattered into different streets. When Stenka Razin thought the right moment had come, he took off his hat and turned it around on his head. This was the signal for his followers to make their attack. Drawing their weapons, they shouted and struck down the strongest Persians near them. Being in the center of eager crowds, they threw the inhabitants into panic. Soon they held all the streets and rushed together into the palace of the governor. Here they found rare treasures from Cathay—porcelain and rock-crystal vessels, carved jade, and fragrant amber.

By then the inhabitants realized that they were the dreaded Cossack raiders. All the surviving people fled. Although the Ataman's band was small, thousands of men ran from them, allowing them to bear off their loot unhindered to the anchored barks.

Well, after that the peace on their island soon came to an end. One drowsy midsummer day fishermen hurried in to the Cossack camps to warn them that a great fleet was coming out from the Persian shore. In fact the Shah had commanded that the robbers—as he thought them—must be wiped out on their island.

His fleet had seventy vessels of all kinds, manned by disciplined soldiers. For a while the Ataman and his lieutenants watched the Persian ships, which moved in slowly because there was almost no wind. The Cossacks were not at all afraid of the size of the vessels or the numbers of the enemy. This was the kind of fighting that suited them best.

Swiftly and skilfully they made ready, the men of the Don, the Volga boatmen, the foresters and the others all doing their share under the Ataman's quick orders. For Stenka Razin was crafty and merciless in a battle.

They put to sea in their long kaiks with driving oars. Some boats had small cannon mounted in the bows; all of them gave out smoke where the forest men were kindling bundles of pinewood torches. They also brought along a few small kegs of powder and all their firearms. They left the larger ships anchored by the island.

That was because the sailing vessels were useless without a wind. You see, the Cossacks knew how to handle every kind of boat on the water, while the Persians who were skilful enough on land did not know much about the sea.

The great sailing ships of the Shah could only drift along. The Cossacks closed in swiftly on both sides of them, firing their muskets and cannon. Half hidden in powder smoke and the smoke of the blazing pine torches, the woodsmen hacked with axes at the water-line of the big vessels. Meanwhile the Volga men put lighted fuses in the powder kegs and hurled them up over the rail among the Persian soldiers, who were shattered by the explosions. Then, throwing the torches before them, the Cossacks swarmed up the sides. Their shout echoed over the still water—*"Sarin na kitchkou!"*

In this way, by attacking a few vessels at a time, the Cossacks became masters of the enemy fleet except for some smaller craft that rowed away in panic. Thousands of Persian soldiers were killed or captured along with their commanders. Thousands of fine shirts

*The Cossacks swarmed up the sides.*

of mail and weapons inlaid with gold fell into the hands of the Ataman's followers.

The Cossacks guarded the Persian nobles carefully,

for they were holding them for ransom. The other prisoners were kept to do the work of slaves.

But two of them the Ataman kept on his own ship. They were the young son and daughter of a Khan of the Persians. The veiled princess made a strange companion to the chief of the Volga pirates. She hid her fear of him and made herself agreeable by bringing him his cups of wine and soothing him by playing skilfully on a guitar when he was in a stormy mood, as often happened.

Stenka Razin came to love this strange girl. He gave her strings of pearls and shining diamonds from his well-filled treasure chest. His men began to think that the Persian slave was bewitching their chief. Filka was jealous of her, and he warned his chief that she would bring ill luck to the ship.

The Ataman said angrily that they had never had such good luck before. But this did not satisfy his men.

No other Persian fleet tried to attack the Cossacks' island. Stenka Razin ruled the Caspian Sea. The story of his deeds was carried to the rivers of the north and to all the people of the steppes.

Probably he might have dwelt safely on his island for years. But he thought of other things—how Krevoi and many officers and brave men had died to gain this victory. When the tall Ataman was troubled in his spirit, he would go off alone to the wet rocks of the shore where seabirds wheeled, crying out. Sometimes an eagle would pass, riding the air currents with out-stretched wings. Then Stenka Razin might hear some of the Cossacks singing, not merrily but softly.

*You are far, Brother Eagle,*
*Far from your home——*
*Far from Mother Volga's shore.*

His surviving Cossacks had more wealth than ever before in their lives. They could go on levying tribute on all this strange sea. Yet few vessels passed over the heavy, gray-green water smelling of oil from the vast oil pits of Baku where everlasting fires smoked and burned.

Stenka Razin understood how his followers longed to be back home again, hunting along their clear rivers where the tall steppe grass smelled of sunlight. He had known that longing when he had been a prisoner in the frozen forests. And he knew, as well, how dangerous it would be for them to go back to the Volga.

One still evening he left the Persian princess at the

shore and strode to the campfires. "Eh, my brothers," he said quietly, "the steppe is our father, the Volga's our mother. Break out the sails—lash up the stores— each one fill his chest. We will sail to our home."

# XI

# ASTRAKHAN

In America the Mississippi was known as the Father of Waters. Smaller rivers flowed into it from the far north. Hunters and Indians could journey by canoe or log raft along these waterways and float down to the sea. At the mouth of the Mississippi the trading town of New Orleans was built. Ships could come in to New Orleans bringing the goods from Europe, while furs and tobacco and other things were brought down the river to sell to merchants who would ship them over the sea to Europe. At that time there were plenty of Indians, French boatmen, and hunters with long squirrel guns coming and going. There were also a few pirates there like Jean Lafitte.

So in this time when Muscovy was becoming the Russian Empire of the Tsars, the mighty Volga flowed through the continent from north to south. From Moscow itself you could sail down the chain of rivers to the Caspian Sea, over which came the merchants of Asia bringing their goods. Hardly any wagon trails had been made through the prairies and the forests, from Moscow as far east as the bare Ural Mountains. Most people journeyed back and forth by water.

And, in the same way that New Orleans guarded the mouth of the Mississippi, the growing city of Astrakhan guarded the mouth of the Volga. Around Astrakhan lay the bazaars of Tartar and Armenian traders, who had sheep and hides, salt and turquoise and other things to sell to the Muscovite merchants who lived within the guarded palisade.

In the middle of Astrakhan rose the high wooden

palace of the Voevode, or Governor—Prince Prozorovsky. This palace had a palisade and cannon of its
own. From his lofty reception room the Voevode could
keep watch over all the city and the river, too. Having
the authority of the Tsar, Prince Prozorovsky could
do pretty much what he liked on this far frontier post.
And the thing he liked best was to collect gifts from
all the merchants and taxes on the goods passing through
Astrakhan.

When Stenka Razin sent messengers to ask for the
Tsar's pardon if his Cossacks returned peacefully to
their homes, Prince Prozorovsky was much pleased. It
almost looked as if he could claim he had brought back
the rebellious Ataman to become a humble subject of
the distant Tsar. But he also meant to extract a heavy
payment for himself from Stenka Razin. He wanted
more money so he could go back to live in luxury at
Moscow.

After thinking all this over, he sent a message to the
Ataman at sea that he had the pardon of Tsar Alexis
all written out and ready to be signed—if Stenka Razin
would give up his cannon and sea-going vessels and a
few other things at Astrakhan. The shrewd Voevode
did not say what those other things were because he

meant to bargain for payment to himself for them.

On his part, Stenka Razin agreed to the terms because his followers had almost no food on their vessels and he wanted to get them safely home past the fleet guarding Astrakhan. But he did not trust the Muscovites. And his men feared that the Persian slave girl would bring ill luck to their Ataman's ship.

When his fleet rowed through the channel to the wooden wall and towers of Astrakhan, he had all his men standing by the loaded cannon. The Voevode had mustered thirty-six vessels and four thousand well-armed Streltsi on the river bank to greet him. The Muscovite soldiery waved flags and fired salutes to honor the Cossacks coming back from their victories in Persia.

In Astrakhan the Cossacks hurried to the markets and spent handfuls of gold for fresh food and new weapons, fishing nets, and all the other articles they needed. The bazaar keepers rejoiced because these Volga men had so much treasure to spend.

Some of the Voevode's foreign officers brought brandy as a gift to Stenka Razin. But the wary Ataman rode through the streets, scattering silver coins to the poor people who rushed to see him. He said he would welcome the illustrious Voevode aboard his own galley to make an agreement with him.

Prince Prozorovsky was astonished when he came out to Stenka Razin's vessel. Silk and satin hung over the rail—soft carpets covered the deck where the visitor and his host sat under a canopy of Chinese silk sewn with gold thread. All the Cossacks swaggered about in shining cloth-of-gold, with jewels sparkling in their belts.

Stenka Razin himself wore a cloak of priceless sables, with a chain of pure gold at his throat. The Persian slave girl poured wine into his goblet. Behind him fiddles played and bagpipes droned, and it looked as if he had need of nothing more. But he needed to have the Tsar's pardon signed.

Warily the two of them bargained. Stenka Razin gave up five of his heaviest brass cannon and twenty iron cannon. He said he needed the other cannon to protect the Cossacks from the Tartars on their way home. And he needed all his vessels to transport his treasure up to Tsaritzin.

When he thought of all the wealth in the ships, Prince Prozorovsky became more eager to bargain. He said the Ataman could keep the captive Persian nobles he was holding for ransom, but he must set free the Streltsi he had forced to join him.

"They were free," retorted Stenka Razin, "from the moment they joined my standard. They can do as they like. It is the Cossack law that those who join us will never be given up."

Then the prince began to admire Stenka Razin's sable cloak, saying it was a fit gift for the Tsar.

"Take it, brother," exclaimed Stenka Razin angrily, throwing off the cloak. "It will do you no good."

"Take care how you speak to me, Stenka Razin," retorted the governor, "for I can do either ill or good for you at Moscow."

But it ended by the Voevode sending the pardon to Moscow to be signed by the Tsar in his mercy. And the Cossacks sailed up the Volga peaceably, being eager to reach their homes. Instead of getting back the soldiers who had joined Stenka Razin, Prince Prozorovsky lost more of his own Streltsi, who deserted to go with the rich Cossacks.

By then great tales of Stenka Razin's magic were heard along the river Volga. The fishermen and peasants heard how bullets struck him and dropped to the

*Warily Razin and Prince Prozorovsky bargained.*

ground without harming his body. Ships sailing against him stopped dead in the water at a word from him. The staff that he always carried acted like a magic wand because it pointed out where treasures had been hidden underground.

There was little truth in these tales. Stenka Razin's triumph had been won by his cunning and daring, and not by the power of magic. But because the river people believed in the power of magic, they believed that Stenka Razin must have that power. And that caused evil to befall him.

One legend tells how he lost the companion he loved, the Persian slave. No sooner were they past Astrakhan than the men of his ship came to him to demand that he send away the girl. They would not have her accompanying them on their river, the Volga.

He had to choose between losing the lovely girl and losing the loyalty of his followers. He could not make up his mind to do either. As usual when his mind was troubled he called for wine to drink. The little princess brought him cup after cup, her eyes pleading wistfully. In anguish, his men say, Stenka Razin leaned against the rail of their bark, looking at nothing but the river. They heard him say to it: "Mother Volga, there is no river like you. All that I am and all that I have gained I owe to you."

Bending low his head, the Ataman said then: "What gift have I ever made to you, Mother Volga? Not a single thing! Now I will give you the thing I love best."

He beckoned to the princess, who of course did not understand what he was saying. He seized her, clad in her silk and pearls and jewels, and flung her far out into the dark water.

The ship sailed on, leaving her to drown in the Volga.

## XII

# THE ATAMAN'S ISLAND

Although Stenka Razin and Prince Prozorovsky had bargained cunningly, they both meant to keep their word to have peace on the Volga. The prince needed the experienced Cossacks to help defend that vast frontier. And Stenka Razin meant to disband his army and let his people seek their homes.

That summer of 1669 his fleet ascended the river from Astrakhan to Tsaritzin without any trouble.

Tsaritzin was a strong frontier post on a high bluff. Its Voevode wanted to close the gates to keep the Cossacks out. But the people who had heard the tales of the Ataman's magic power rushed out to complain to him. They said the governor had taken horses and grain from them when they did not have coins enough to pay the taxes. Without horses they could not haul their carts; without grain they could have no bread in winter.

The Ataman listened to these peasants and fishermen, and then went up into the log town. His Cossacks swarmed into the taverns to buy vodka and corn brandy. They found that the tavern keepers of Tsaritzin charged double the just price for such spirits. That was by order of the Voevode, who hoped to keep some of the money for himself after paying the tax on the spirits to Moscow.

This enraged Stenka Razin, who remembered how he himself had been treated in the tavern at Moscow.

"Break down all doors!" he shouted.

The first thing his Cossacks did was to break open the doors of the prison and let loose all the captives of the Voevode. Next they broke into the Voevode's guarded house. But he had slipped out the back way and was hiding in a watchman's hut. The Cossacks searched, sword in hand, until they found him. By then they were merry with so much sport, and Stenka Razin forbade them to burn the hut with the governor in it. So they did something else; each time a Cossack filled up his goblet, he strode into the hut and pulled the Voevode's beard. And the people of Tsaritzin forced him to pay back in silver coins the money he had been squeezing from them. They could do this because now everyone on the lower Volga feared the power of Stenka Razin.

Because of this trouble at Tsaritzin, the Ataman did not give up to the Muscovites the sea-going barks of his fleet as he had promised Prince Prozorovsky to do. These barks were too big to haul over the portage to the river Don.

When the Cossacks made their way across the portage, near Stenka Razin's old home, they carted over their kaiks and remaining treasures. And the prisoners who had been freed in Tsaritzin went along. All the way, fisher folk and prairie hunters joined the Cossacks, bringing their women with them. They had heard how the tall Ataman managed to care for all the poor and the homeless who joined him.

It was the end of autumn then, with the sun warm on the brown steppe grass—the time we call Indian summer. The wild geese were winging their way south. And Stenka Razin found a home for his people on the quiet Don, on a long island where they could defend themselves against attack.

Here at the island of Kagalnik each family built the kind of house it wanted—roofed with sailcloth or dry, woven grass. The hunters went out before daybreak along the banks, and the fishermen set their nets in the narrows of the tranquil river. Everyone felt merry because they had meat to roast at the fires in the evening. They repeated an old saying of the steppes: "A horse has four legs, and I have four things—meat and brandy, good boots, and Saint Nicholas to watch over me."

The Cossack warriors took no thought for the next day. But the women, who knew the dangers of the frontier, worked anxiously to have things for the next days. They pickled the fish in brine, and beat the milk in sacks into sour cream, and spun the wool of the sheep into threads to make clothing.

When he had a house made of willow poles and

dried clay, Stenka Razin sent one of his trusted lieutenants, Ivan Boldir, to bring his mother to his new town of Kagalnik. His mother had grown old, but she still worked hard at making the rooms clean and white with dry lime and water. Secretly she blessed the charm of the kolduna who had sworn so long ago that her son would never be harmed by bullets or steel.

With her she brought the girl Alena, who had been waiting for Stenka Razin to come home. Alena had helped him ride herd when he was young. She had eyes for no other man than the son of Timofe. For years she had scarcely seen him, so she had helped his mother instead.

"*Ekh-ma*," his mother sighed. "He cherishes only his sword. He will never take thought for a wife."

Still, the old woman and the girl were happy at Kagalnik, for Stenka Razin meant to dwell in peace in this town.

Even when snow covered the steppe, and they had only smoked fish and black bread to eat, more and more people sought refuge on the island. Blind musicians felt their way thither, to sing of the Ataman's deeds; gypsy bands drifted there with their gay head cloths and music of flutes and cymbals and bell staffs.

*Stenka Razin meant to dwell in peace in this town.*

Tartar herdsmen brought in their sheep and by the fires they danced their wild *Tsingra* to the gypsy music. When night fell they shouted "*Aia-a—hiha— aihaa!*" This was to keep evil spirits away from their herds.

And from far Solovetsky monastery, the stout monk Chvedor led a strange pilgrimage to Kagalnik. He was fatter and merrier than ever. The folk with him were throngs of the Old Believers. They wanted to find some new land where they could chant their old prayers and build a church for their ikons of St. Nicholas and St. George the Deliverer. Stenka Razin bade them do as they liked on his island.

"God and Allah are the same to me," he said, after thinking it over. "What are priests good for except to marry young couples? Pray as you wish, Old Believers."

So more bands of the Old Believers sought his island. For these few weeks it looked as if the Ataman of the Homeless might build a great city in the steppes for his people. Foreign princes sent envoys to greet him, because of his power. Merchant caravans coming up the Don stopped to trade at Kagalnik where so much treasure was to be gained.

Then, with the warmth of spring, trouble came to the island on the Don.

## XIII

# REVOLT IN THE
# STEPPES

In Moscow the Tsar Alexis had a kind heart, and perhaps he wanted most of all to do the right things for
the many different peoples under his rule. Yet most of
the time he was shut up in the walls of the Kremlin.
He heard of what happened on the far frontiers only
through spies or the great boyars who governed for

him out there. Never could he go about among the peasants and rivermen like Stenka Razin.

So in his great pillared audience hall, where guards held axes before him and secretaries wrote down every word spoken, Alexis listened to the nobles who bowed their heads at his feet. They told him that the masterless men of the steppes had forgotten their fear of God and their obedience to their Lord the Tsar—they had robbed merchants and made war on the Persians, and pulled the beards of his governors.

When Cossack envoys came from Stenka Razin all the way to Moscow to get the signed pardon of the Tsar, Alexis asked them who had stirred them up to such deeds.

Now the Cossacks of Kagalnik had the custom of speaking only the truth in a council. Here in Moscow, they did as they had always done in the Rada of their own people. They bent their shaven heads in thought and pulled at their long mustaches. Then the eldest of them lifted his head and explained.

"It was like this, our father, the Tsar. On the Don our people hungered. To get food we could not go upon the Black Sea, where the chain of the Turks barred our way. Therefore we went down the Volga to

the Caspian Sea. We did this without the will of Yakublev, the Ataman of the Don Cossacks. Nay—our
leader in all that happened was Stenka, son of Timofe
Razin."

After the Cossacks had spoken in this way, the
boyars told something very different to Alexis. The
priests of the Kremlin churches told how throngs of
Old Believers had left their villages to flee to Stenka
Razin. Then powerful landowners, the boyars of Muscovy, complained that many of their serfs were escaping from their lawful lands and seeking the roads to
Kagalnik.

At that time the peasants who tilled the farms in
Muscovy had been forbidden to go to any other place.
So they had become like slaves who could do nothing
except labor for their masters—as serfs. By trying to
flee to the wilderness they broke the law of Muscovy.

Now the Cossack envoys had kept their eyes open
around them. When they returned that spring to Kagalnik they related to Stenka Razin how strife stirred
the lands around Moscow. Whether they brought back
with them the signed pardon of the Tsar nobody
knows. Because trouble began just then in all the
steppes.

What happened was that the boyars who surrounded Alexis sent envoys hurriedly into the prairie lands to work against the power of the Ataman of the Golytba. One envoy reproached Prince Prozorovsky for not getting back the Streltsi. Another took presents across the Volga to the great Khan of the Kalmuks, urging him not to let Stenka Razin into his lands. Another hastened down the Don to the head man Yakublev, to threaten him with the Tsar's anger for aiding Stenka Razin.

The last envoy was a Swedish officer in the pay of Moscow who dared go to Kagalnik itself. There he came face to face with Stenka Razin.

This Swedish captain was indeed a bold man. First he showed the Cossacks a scroll signed in red ink by Alexis. Then he gave his message: "In the name of your master the Tsar, release all men you have taken from his service into your own. Be warned! If you disobey this command, or break the laws again, you will have no second pardon granted you. Nay, Cossack, you will be judged for your crimes."

At this the giant Ataman grew hot with rage. "Who hired such a fool," he roared, "to bid me give up my children?" He tore open his coat of cloth-of-gold, showing the letters branded on his chest—C A I N. "They named me well, did your masters. Go and tell them! I will let the blood out of their bodies before I will give up one man of mine."

The officer became pale and silent, but he held his head high. The quick-witted Filka stepped before the raging Stenka Razin, while other lieutenants led the Swede away. They all knew that an envoy who came with a message must not be harmed.

Filka tried to make Stenka Razin think of something else. "This foreigner obeys an order—but who gives the order?" he muttered. "Eh, Ataman, up at Cherkask the Muscovites are threatening the elders of the Don. What say you to that?"

Instead of answering, Stenka Razin strode out to the horselines. Taking a sheepskin coat from a Cossack, he climbed to the saddle of a swift horse and galloped toward Cherkask, the headquarters of the fighting men of the Don. In his anger he stopped only to change horses. His lieutenants who tried to keep up with him soon fell behind.

Alone, Stenka Razin rode into the town of Cherkask where the battle standards of the Host of the Don were kept.

*"They named me well, did your masters!"*

He strode into the circle of the standing warriors. There the old Ataman, Yakublev, was trying to appease the proud envoy from Moscow. When they saw Stenka Razin's scarred face, everyone was silent.

He looked around at all of them and drew from his belt his ivory baton. "Cossacks, brothers of the Don," Stenka Razin shouted, "I have heard too much old women's talk! Now listen to me."

Without hesitating a moment, he called for an end to the council of the Don Ataman, Yakublev, and he called for a new council of Stenka Razin, Ataman of the Homeless. When this was done he asked them if they meant to be ruled by the lords of Moscow and bow down in fear, or to rule themselves as their fathers had done.

"Nay," cried the Muscovite noble, "it is the Tsar your father who summons you to obey!"

"Not the Tsar!" retorted Stenka Razin. "The boyars, the slave-masters, the lords of the Kremlin. And this one," he snarled at the richly robed envoy, "will spit out no more lies."

With his fist he smashed the Muscovite to the ground. By then some of his own fighting men had ridden into the council. At his command they picked up the Muscovite and hurled him into the flooded, ice-flecked river. The body disappeared into the waters.

Old Yakublev protested that this act would bring an army from Moscow to avenge it.

Yakublev spoke for the elder Cossacks of Cherkask who were weary of war and had great estates and herds of their own. Scarred Stenka Razin spoke for the homeless and refugees. He spoke with anger of his brother's death. He gave a great laugh and tossed up his ivory staff for all to see.

"We are dogs, Yakublev, to bite the boyars. Ay, we are hunting hounds to track down their armies. Who will hunt with me?"

The younger men sided with Stenka Razin, the elders with Yakublev. Tidings of the revolt sped over the steppes, out to the Volga. Riders swept from hamlet to hamlet, shouting that the Ataman of the Homeless would stand against the Muscovites—Stenka Razin would ride against Moscow.

"Let the Tsar rule in Moscow," the riders said. "The Cossacks will rule the Don."

It was not wise for Stenka Razin to plan to do any such thing. But the warriors of Cherkask, the peasants and fisherfolk of Kagalnik, and the Volga boatmen begged him to do it.

When the floods receded in the rivers and the grass was good for grazing, Stenka Razin marched from his town of Kagalnik.

His mother and the girl Alena put on their brightest kerchiefs and carried out a tray with fresh new bread and wine to refresh him before he mounted his horse. Then they went back into their new home to wait.

# XIV

# THE TRAP ON THE RIVER

It was really no rebellion at all. The people who followed Stenka Razin had dwelt on the frontier for many generations. They believed that they owned the prairies and the rivers, while the powerful Muscovites were strangers who came with soldiers to enforce their orders.

The Khan of the Kalmuks, for instance, did not want to submit to the orders from Moscow unless he had to. It did not seem possible to the wily nomad Khan that one man could defy Moscow. Yet because he wanted Stenka Razin to win the victory he sent horse herds to the Cossacks, to aid them. He said his father had sworn friendship with the men of the Don and Volga, and they had poured water on their swords. The ignorant peasants, however, thought that Stenka Razin's magic had brought this about.

As soon as he had horses enough for all his hunters and warriors, the Ataman led them swiftly out on the portage trail to the Volga. Far up the river, keen-eyed boatmen had been keeping watch for him. Some of these watchers hurried downstream in a swift-sailing sloop to warn him that two regiments of Muscovite infantry were coming down to Tsaritzin to hold that town against him.

Stenka Razin knew that he had no time to lose. In two days he moved swiftly across the portage. And he sent several hunters ahead with the merry monk Chvedor, who did not look at all like a rebel. Stout Chvedor tied the skirt of his black robe about his middle and rode without stopping to sleep.

When he entered the gate of Tsaritzin he went straight to a tavern with his companions. Men crowded in to ask for tidings of what was happening. Then Chvedor whispered that Stenka Razin was leading all the people of the Don over to celebrate his victories with the good folk of Tsaritzin. So, said the merry monk, they ought to parade out to honor him, and show their joy. For if the gates were shut against him the Ataman would be angered and fire with his cannon.

Most of the people agreed with the monk as to the best thing to do. While the anxious Voevode and the garrison prepared to defend the walls, the people flung open the gates and ran out, singing and holding up the holy ikons, or pictures, of their church to show that they welcomed the Ataman of the Homeless.

When they did this, Stenka Razin lost no time in riding in to Tsaritzin with his experienced Cossacks. The Voevode and his soldiery had to retire to the citadel on the height. The Cossacks rode their horses close under the wooden wall and braced their lances against the parapet. From the horses the young Cossacks swarmed up the lances while others threw blazing torches over their heads. They broke into the citadel and dragged out the Voevode. The townspeople, who hated him, cast him into the river at the end of a rope. Then they pulled him to and fro until he drowned.

Stenka Razin laughed at this, and praised the monk Chvedor. "*Eh, batko,*" he said, "well, little father, you have more wit than my captains, because you have captured this town by a jest."

Chvedor shook his head. "Then send me to Moscow, Ataman," he begged. "For you and your men will never be safe from the Muscovites until you capture their city."

But the Chief of the Cossacks faced a danger much nearer than Moscow. Spies reported the flotilla of soldiers approaching Tsaritzin.

Stenka Razin knew that these were disciplined soldiers led by skilled foreign officers. They could not be tricked by Chvedor. So he and Filka and Vaska Usk prepared a trap for the Muscovite fleet of longboats. After closing the gates of Tsaritzin, they sent the best of the Cossacks mounted on good horses up the river bank. Filka gave the Old Believers matchlock guns he had seized, and led them with most of the others by boat up the river itself. Stenka Razin waited on the wall of lofty Tsaritzin with some men who could work the cannon.

By dividing up in this manner, they did not let it appear how numerous they were. The Muscovite flotilla hurried downstream, anxious only to reach Tsaritzin and unaware that the Cossacks had seized the town. First the soldiers met the longboats of Filka, which fired on them from near the opposite shore. Then suddenly the veteran mounted Cossacks appeared on the near bank, firing at the backs of the soldiers. Under fire from both sides, the Muscovites rowed hard in mid-stream toward the town.

But when they reached the landing, the cannon of Stenka Razin blasted at them from the parapets. At the same time Filka's flotilla closed in to the landing behind the soldiers who were thrown into disorder. At that moment the mounted Cossacks charged along the bank into them with leveled lances and flailing swords. Only three hundred soldiers were left alive when the Muscovites surrendered. These prisoners were given the choice of pulling an oar or serving the Ataman.

"Here we have no boyars or serfs," Stenka Razin told them. "We have only the brotherhood of the Cossacks, to share the danger and the plunder."

His men had a new battle cry: "For God and Allah, and our Tsar and the Cossack Host!"

For Stenka Razin still believed he was serving the far-off Tsar.

Chvedor wanted to hurry up the river, to win over all the frontier towns—all the way to Moscow. While Stenka Razin meditated this, he heard that Prince Prozorovsky was leading the fleet of Astrakhan up against him. To make an example of the rebels, as he called them, the Prince had tortured a Cossack spy to death and hung his mangled body on the mast of the foremost galley.

This news decided the Ataman to turn down the river to meet his antagonist the Prince. Perhaps he would have done better to go toward Moscow where multitudes of people were hailing him as their chief.

As it was, he led his new host of eight thousand men in boats down the Volga. In his anger at Prince Prozorovsky, he was blind to anything else.

When the two fleets met, no battle took place. Almost all the Streltsi of the Prince put aside their guns and shouted that they would join the Ataman of the Homeless. The Muscovite noble had to escape in his own galley back to Astrakhan.

*The mounted Cossacks charged along the bank.*

The next town the Cossacks seized by one of their stratagems. A number of them dressed up in the green-and-red uniforms of the Streltsi who had joined them. Clad in this way, like Muscovites they were able to march right into the palisade.

Now the way was clear to Astrakhan. But that city guarding the Volga mouths had a high wall of logs and earth, with more than four hundred brass cannon. And it was under command of the Prince, who now regretted that he had ever allowed Stenka Razin to come back to the Volga.

## XV

# THE END OF PRINCE
# PROZOROVSKY

As it happened, in that June of the year 1670 the Muscovites had thought of building a navy for themselves. You see, the men of Moscow had no vessels large enough or sound enough to voyage out on the seas.

The first ship they launched was a small bark

named the *Orel* or Eagle. With brass cannon mounted on its deck, the *Orel* sailed down the Volga. Foreign officers commanded the little ship, because at that time the Muscovites had not learned how to do so. That spring the *Orel* was moored to a dock on the island where Astrakhan stood.

So the foreign officers beheld what happened at Astrakhan when the Cossacks appeared. A Dutch merchant heard the people talking about the new Chief of the Cossacks whom they described as the Liberator. "They called him Father," Jean Struys, the merchant, relates. "He made himself feared and also loved by many."

By then Prince Prozorovsky himself had begun to fear Stenka Razin. He tried to make sure of the loyalty of his own soldiers by handing out to them large sums of rubles which he took from the churches. Then he had all the cannon put in place on the great wooden wall of the city. He had all the large gates closed and barred and then sealed with brick walls inside. After that he rode through the streets in his gilt chain armor, with his banner following, giving out spears and axes to the crowds of peasants and artisans, urging them to fight with him for the Tsar.

The people had been grumbling ever since they saw some spies of the Cossacks tortured to death. The Prince who governed them was a little afraid of his own people as the fleet of Stenka Razin drew nearer. So he put the foreign officers, whom he trusted, in command at the gates—flattering them and making them gifts of costly garments.

A young Scot, David Butler, served for pay as ensign on the anchored *Orel*. "The Governor ordered me to take charge of all the cannon," David Butler relates. "We fetched ashore the gear and ammunition from our ship, and loaded the cannon on the wall. I made the rounds of the fortifications with an English colonel.

"When we came in, the Governor asked how we thought the city could best be defended. For my part, I advised that we offer pardon to all who had joined the rebellion, and rewards to their leaders. But my advice was not followed.

"On the fifteenth of June we dined at the Governor's table and afterwards he gave me a fine satin robe. He promoted me to be Lieutenant and posted me where the city wall was weakest.

"That same day the Cossacks came in sight. They

sent a man and a priest to summon the city to surrender. These also brought a letter to me written in German, advising me to do nothing myself if I wished to live. The Governor tore his letter in two, and at once ordered the two envoys to be beheaded.

"The next day some three hundred sloops of the enemy sailed in to a vineyard half a league from the city. We gave out a hogshead of strong beer to the soldiers, with some tobacco. That night, after making the round of the ramparts with two of my fellows, I threw myself down on a mattress to sleep for an hour or two."

(While David Butler slept, the Cossacks were stealing through the orchards, creeping into the empty bazaar of the Tartars—who had ridden off into the desert to escape the danger. Imitating the call of night birds, the Cossacks attracted the attention of the expectant townspeople, some of whom let down ladders from the ramparts. Then out of the alleys crept the throngs Prince Prozorovsky had armed with rude weapons. Most of the soldiers on guard decided to put down their arms and stay where they were. Only the foreign officers, by then, were willing to fight and they did not suspect what was going on.)

"Someone woke me," David Butler relates, "saying that the rebels were coming to attack at the gate. I could make out a company of them drawing near. Then I began to fire off our cannon. The only one who came to help me was Thomas Bailly, the English colonel, armed with a breastplate, with several German officers. He told me we were betrayed—and he had been injured in the face when he tried to make his soldiers resist the attack.

"Although treason was clearly all about us, I pretended not to believe it. I advised him to go back to his post. He went back with the others. At first their soldiers seemed to be ready to carry out their orders. But an hour later I was told they had all been massacred by their men. At the same time a German captain standing very near me was seized by his servants and tied and then killed.

"This sight frightened the Surgeon who was with me then. He wanted, in spite of me, to jump from the parapet of the wall to the ground to escape. I stopped him by saying I knew a better way than that.

"I had noticed a sally door at the base of a tower, very near. To this I led him with his valet, and two of my crew. At the door the sentries recognized me and let us pass—the Surgeon first and then me. But we saw nothing more of the valet and the sailors.

"As soon as we were out, we plunged into the water up to our necks to try to reach the Tartar market, which would be our best chance of safety—guiding ourselves by the musket shots overhead."

(However, Lieutenant Butler did not manage to escape. By then the Cossacks and the armed mob had cornered the governor, Prozorovsky, with his bodyguard and foreign officers near one of the gates. There the Swedish captain who had braved Stenka Razin at Kagalnik was killed. Prozorovsky sounded his trumpets for aid from his soldiers on the wall. But none of them came to help him. The nobles and officials around him were cut down, and his bodyguards killed. In spite of his fine armor the Prince was wounded, and dragged to the cathedral church where other Muscovites had taken refuge. They were all overcome and tied up against the walls, to wait for the judgment of Stenka Razin. When the giant Ataman appeared in the smoke of flaming torches, he asked if Prozorovsky gave himself up. The wounded Prince shook his head. Then Stenka Razin carried him up the high bell tower of the church and flung him to the ground to die. He had

*The* Orel, *the first ship of the Russian navy.*

been too proud of his own power, but he had been a brave man.)

(In this way Stenka Razin became master of mighty Astrakhan and all the wealth of its Muscovite merchants. Only a handful of his Cossacks had lost their lives in capturing the city. Because some Cossacks had been tortured by the Muscovite officials, many of these were flung into the river by the victorious men of the steppes—others were thrown from the ramparts upon great steel hooks fixed in the walls, and left there to die like speared fish. When Stenka Razin had been drinking, he could be as cruel as any of his outlaws; at other times he would have no hand in the slaughter of the Muscovites. On the second day young David Butler and his friend the Surgeon were taken before Stenka Razin for judgment, both of them weak and half starved after their capture.)

"In the evening, about six o'clock, we were taken before Razin, Chief of the Cossacks." So Lieutenant Butler explained what befell him. "This Chief demanded of the Surgeon who he was. Finding out, he sent him to attend to the wounded, promising him his life.

"Razin asked me the same question, and the Surgeon answered for me that I was his comrade. At this they took him away.

" 'But you,' Stenka Razin persisted, 'what do you know how to do?'

"I said nothing, because the Surgeon who had spoken for me well had claimed me for his friend. I stood there alone, thinking they would kill me.

"Razin was sitting in the street in front of the Bishop's house, drinking with his officers. They were as drunk as he or almost so. They questioned a Muscovite colonel and sentenced him to be thrown from the

tower whence the Governor had been thrown . . .
Hardly an hour passed that I did not see someone die.
They fixed a hook in the side of the Secretary, Alexis,
and hung him up by it. . . .

"While I waited my turn, Stenka Razin kept looking at me steadily. I was on the point of falling down
from weakness. He ordered some spirits to be given
me. Two mugs of this drink refreshed me comfortably.
I was able to walk over to his armed men where at the
end he ordered me to go.

"They took me to a boat near that of the Chief and
fed me. Soon he left Astrakhan, taking the swarm of
boats with him."

In this way David Butler lived to tell of his meeting
with the dreaded Ataman. When he sailed away, Stenka
Razin took with him the captured *Orel*, the first ship
of the Russian navy. But he did not need any foreign
officers to work the small vessel. His Cossacks could
do that well enough.

## XVI

# COSSACK REPUBLIC

Before leaving Astrakhan, Stenka Razin did a surprising thing. He called for an assembly of all the people. This was not the council of the elder Cossacks but the ancient *viech* or assembly of all the headmen of the land—very much like the gathering of our Congress a century later.

130

To this viech came the representatives of the Volga burlaki, the Tartar tribesmen, the townsmen, and even the Armenian and Persian merchants whom the Ataman had protected from harm. And of course his folk of Kagalnik and the Don Cossacks had their spokesmen, too.

When he faced them all Stenka Razin explained that henceforth they must till the farmlands, and carry on trade up and down the river. They must repair the damage to Astrakhan, and guard themselves from attack. No longer would the Muscovites give them orders.

In this way they would rule themselves, Cossack fashion. They would be a Cossack Republic, swearing allegiance only to Stenka Razin and the Tsar.

To govern Astrakhan he left Vaska Usk, now growing old. To guard the town, he left one man in five of his hardy Cossacks, and one man in two of the Streltsi of Astrakhan who had joined his standard.

Most of the treasure he had captured Stenka Razin sent on thirty vessels to be taken to Kagalnik where it would be safe.

He could have stayed in command here at the far edge of the Caspian Sea, and held his power unchallenged. But every day messengers arrived from the north, begging him to come swiftly and free the people there.

Now Stenka Razin had learned only how to keep his people alive on his prairies. Even Chvedor had taught him nothing of book learning. When families in need came to their Ataman to borrow money for seed grain or harvesting tools, he did not lend but gave away what he had. So the people of every kind came to love him. Yet he really understood only how to fight, not to govern wisely. As long as his domain lay upon the Volga itself he was invincible.

But the vast lands of the Russian Empire awaited him in the north where new armies of Muscovites were mustering that summer.

When he began his journey into Muscovy hundreds of boats came out to join him, bringing gifts of salted fish and dried fruit. Hunters went out at dawn along the banks to bring in game for the next camp up the river. Thousands of his veteran Cossacks rode up the shore beside his fleet, collecting barley and sour cream and cabbages for soup from the frontier villages. In fact all Stenka Razin's gathering host took care of itself on the journey north because his people had always fared for themselves on this frontier.

The powerful Kalmuk Khan rode in to the bank with his warriors moving like wind through the sea of grass. The shrewd eyes of the nomad Khan surveyed the power of the marching Cossacks, and he was satisfied to be the friend of the Ataman.

At the portage to the Don, the women of Kagalnik waited to watch him pass, hoping that he would return to his island and make an end of war. Perhaps if he had done so, Stenka Razin might have ruled the rivers for a long time. But he scarcely paused for a night to take on his vessels the food the women had prepared for him. His aged mother came with Alena to watch with pride and anxiety the tall figure of the beloved Ataman. His mother, with the Tartar blood, rejoiced because she thought the spell laid on him after birth had shielded him from bullets and the stroke of steel. Certainly he had not been wounded.

Boldly she begged him to return to rule his city of Kagalnik. Alena could not beg like that, because a young woman might not speak out to an Ataman commanding warriors on the march.

Stenka Razin laughed gayly at his worried mother. "God alone gives! Sometimes a Cossack rides in the saddle—sometimes he walks, carrying the saddle."

Sailing on, standing proudly under the crimson canopy by the steering sweep of his galley, the giant Ataman was merry that summer.

As far as his keen eyes could see in all directions the grasslands belonged to his Republic. At the end of the plains Saratov opened its gates to him, and fitted out boats to join him. Where white chalk cliffs lined the right bank and the dark forests began, Samara greeted him as Chief. There the Voevode and the garrison had been slain. This was an old city of the Golden Horde, with vast herds of cattle. Half of them Stenka Razin took with him when he sailed on.

"At the end of the river," Stenka Razin told the stout monk Chvedor, "we will sail to Moscow, and ride into it."

"Then may Saint Nicholas aid us," sighed the monk, sipping his wine. "For this river does not lead to Moscow."

Nor was the multitude of hopeful people now following Stenka Razin—a hundred thousand, it is said—

*His aged mother begged him to return to his city.*

an army trained to do battle on land like the Muscovite.

Just at that time, as the fatal summer drew toward its end, the men of Moscow struck their first blow at Stenka Razin himself.

## XVII

## THE ASSASSINS

Naturally, Moscow had become alarmed at the approach of Stenka Razin. The Tsar Alexis and his courtiers, his boyars and military commanders, all consulted together as to what they should do.

You see, Great Russia—the part all around Moscow —lay far inland within forests often closed up by heavy winter snow. Then, too, ice filled most of the nearest seas in the north by the monastery of Solovetsky. So Moscow depended mostly on the trade and traffic that came up the mighty river Volga. Now Stenka Razin had become master of the southern part of the Volga.

But more than that, he had roused up the old peoples of the land against Moscow. His Cossack Republic, although a rude makeshift, was a very different kind of government than the rule of Moscow. It is true that Moscow educated the ordinary people in its schools, yet it made most of them labor as serfs under armed guard.

That summer all kinds of rumors filled the streets of Moscow of the White Wall. Because of the troubles, the harvest failed and there was hunger within the city. The priests of the Kremlin announced that Stenka Razin was no Ataman of the Homeless but a man doing the evil work of the Devil. Some older people who did not understand what was happening went out to a gate to welcome the Chief of the Cossacks with bread and salt. They were seized and a leg and an arm cut off each one. After that their bodies were hung up in the

Red Place for the crowds to see, and it was said that they had wanted to bring the Devil into Moscow.

Anxious nobles, however, like the general, Prince Dolgoruki—who had hanged Stenka Razin's brother for disobedience—knew that they must break the Ataman's power over the common people. The surest way to do that was to contrive to kill him. So two spies were given handfuls of gold ducats and promised more if they succeeded in slaying the leader of the revolt. The two dressed themselves in the sheepskins of Tartars. Each one had a flintlock pistol hidden inside his coat. Swiftly they journeyed down the river Oka to the south.

By chance they found Stenka Razin visiting the white domed tents of one of the older peoples. These were the Cheremiss, a wild folk who hunted among the thin birch forests. They wore the skins of animals even in summer, and had only bows and arrows for weapons. But they were skilled hunters, eager to go with the giant Ataman against the Muscovites who had built log forts in their land.

It was near the end of the long summer evening. Stenka Razin sat brooding on a great white bearskin by the fire of the Cheremiss chieftains. He watched the young warriors doing a fire dance before him—throwing torches into the air and to each other as they leaped in the dance. He took no notice of the pair of assassins disguised as Tartars.

However, a real Tartar of the Volga crouched in the shadow behind him. This was Zamurza, a wizened wild-ox hunter who could track a beast through dry grass. He had made his body a shield for Stenka Razin by sleeping through the night on the deck before the Ataman's cabin.

Old Zamurza carried a curved knife in his girdle, its edge whetted sharp so it could sever a strand of silk. He noticed how the two strange Tartars pushed their way to the front row of the crouching throng. They looked like two ordinary visitors.

When Stenka Razin rose to his great height to make his talk to the Cheremiss chieftains, the two assassins exchanged a glance. At the stir in the listening crowd, a large bird winged its way over the fire—a crane seeking a new resting place. Yet to the Tartar, Zamurza, this was a sign of danger. Swiftly his glance went around him, searching for anything unwonted or ominous.

Stenka Razin was pouring a little milk from the bowl in his hand, first to the north, then to the south, and then toward the place of the sun's rising and setting. This was a greeting to the invisible spirits of the forest-land that the tribesmen reverenced. Then he spoke: "*Allahim barabat yik saftir,*" he murmured. "God alone is just and merciful." That was the usual prayer of the Tartars.

It seemed to the watching Zamurza that the two newcomers did not listen. All the others understood Stenka Razin, but these two did not seem to understand.

Zamurza stiffened and moved silently nearer the fire. *Why,* he wondered silently, *did not these two understand the speech of their country?*

"*Yarou!*" old Zamurza called out suddenly. This meant—"Look out!"

As he spoke he drew out a large stick burning in the fire. This he moved over the ground, closer to the knees of the crouching strangers. Stenka Razin turned to look at him.

"There is a snake in the grass," Zamurza muttered. Of course he had seen no snake but he was suspicious of the two unknown men.

Probably they were alarmed when people began to glance their way. They did not know what Zamurza was saying. Quickly they pulled the pistols from their girdles inside the coats. Hastily they pointed the weapons at Stenka Razin.

Zamurza flung his smoldering stick at their heads. The two shots exploded, and smoke swirled toward the Ataman.

He did not move. The bullets had missed him and disappeared into the trees. At this the Cheremiss made an outcry and seized the assassins, who tried vainly to escape.

To the watching people it seemed that Stenka Razin's magic had made the flying bullets harmless.

"Tie up the dogs," he ordered his followers. "Send them back to Moscow as our gift."

This order Zamurza carried out in a fearsome way of his own.

"They will feed the wolves," he said, "who were wolves themselves."

By then, at the end of the summer, there was no mercy shown by either side in the struggle for Moscow.

*Zamurza flung his smoldering stick at their heads.*

## XVIII

## THE LAST FESTIVAL

By the time harvesting began, it looked as if Stenka Razin's power would triumph in Muscovy itself. Even during the war, these people in the north had to hurry to reap their grain before frost set in. And Stenka Razin told them this time they were free to keep all the harvest for themselves. To prove his words he ordered a *Yarmarok* or Harvest Fair to be held on the river.

All his growing fleet was drawn up along the shore of the Volga. The large ships like the captured *Orel* were anchored with flying banners. Meat sizzled over great fires and wine casks stood open for all to drink, as the Ataman sat in the sable cloak that he had found again in Astrakhan. Because his galley shone with red velvet, people who did not know him said that this must be the vessel of the *Gusodar*—the Lord King. Surely he was more than an Ataman of the Homeless. Because the galley of the monk Chvedor was draped in black satin, the people thought it must be carrying the Patriarch of the Church.

Neither Chvedor nor Filka troubled to tell them the truth. The more the common folk looked up to Stenka Razin the better it would be, they thought.

The Cheremiss hunters helped bring food to this great Fair of the Cossacks. Bands of another strange people, the Chuvash, came from the river Oka in canoes to join Stenka Razin. These were small, silent men resembling the Finns. With them they brought the wooden image of St. Nicholas that they worshipped. When the harvests were good, these Chuvash patted the image and prayed to it; when things went wrong they whipped it with branches. As gifts to the Cossack Chief they offered horses stolen from the Muscovite villages.

From the pine forest came the tall, red-haired Mordvas. Like the others they were the older inhabitants of the land, eager to drive out the colonists from Moscow.

By now it seemed as if all those who dwelt on the rivers or the forests or the prairies were marching on Moscow of the mighty walls.

Unseen tribal hunters flitted through the mist to drive the cattle from the Muscovite villages. Volga boatmen stole up at night to cut anchored vessels from the quays.

Because of this peril on the river, Muscovite merchants tried to send their goods by wagon train along the narrow forest trails. But the spies of the Cossacks, watching from haystacks and tall treetops, sent word of the moving trains and when they stopped for the night bands of invisible men stole off with their loads. When stagecoaches carrying officers or boyars tried to hurry to outlying towns, galloping Don Cossacks often overtook them. After stripping the passengers to the skin, the men of the Don left them to walk home barefoot.

"Alas," a governor wrote to his Minister in Moscow, "no wolves ever troubled us like these brigands. Nor does any supply of food reach us from the river."

At times blind bandura players appeared at the gate of a governor's castle to beg for their supper. They seemed to be helpless folk, but they put new words to their familiar songs:

> *Harken, my brothers!*
> *Like a whirlwind,*
> *He casts no shadow before him!*
> *Like the lightning,*
> *He makes no sound.*
> *Like the flood in its course,*
> *He gives no warning.*
> *Look up, my brothers, for his coming.*

They were messengers of Stenka Razin.

Other messengers galloped headlong along the trails to Kazan. (This had been the city of the Tartars before Ivan the Terrible conquered it.) They proclaimed that the Tartar merchants of Kazan could rule their city again. Many of them gave goods to aid the Cossacks and be free of the taxes and tolls of Muscovy.

On the river Dnieper, Stenka Razin's messengers sped to the encampment of the Hetman Doroshenko. He had rebelled also, to join the Krim Khan and seek the aid of the Turks.

At Nijni Novgorod, close to Moscow, a rider tossed a pole with a horsetail over the wall, and the people made ready to open their gates at the approach of Stenka Razin.

Rumors of his coming sprang up everywhere. There were no newspapers, of course, in Muscovy at that time. The only official news came by order from the bureaus of Moscow. For most tidings the villagers depended on what travelers told them, or what they heard at distant crossroads. And Filka and Chvedor took care to spread tales of the power of the Ataman of the Homeless.

They knew that this silent battle to give hope to people and stir fear in their enemies was more important than any battle of guns and charging horses. It had always been that way in Russia where the multitudes had little means of judging matters for themselves.

Even in far Solovetsky, the monks talked it over

among themselves, and cast out their superior from Moscow. They said they wanted a Cossack Republic in their monastery!

During all this the giant Ataman was gathering his forces on the upper Volga. At the Fair to which such multitudes thronged he gave away not only food but coins and weapons as well. When the young maidens of the Mordva folk appeared at his galley, his Cossacks laughed at the strange girls with slim white-bandaged legs under their short black skirts. "*Hai*, little Swans," the warriors called at them. Stenka Razin, however, gave a pearl taken from his treasure chests to each maiden.

An old Cossack woman, watching this from the shore, drew her kerchief over her head, as if grieving. Stenka Razin noticed that and went over to her. "Eh, little mother," he said, "why do you weep at the sight of pearls?"

This Cossack woman who had come all the way from Kagalnik looked up at him, shaking her gray head. "Don't you know, Ataman, that the tears of mothers are like to pearls?"

Grieving, she told him why that was. "The blind

bandura players know that once, after a battle, Our Lady of the Encampment came down from the sky to walk through the Cossack land. Good Saint Nicholas was guiding her. After she had walked for a little Our Lady became thirsty.

"Listen to what happened. She went first to one door, then to another door of a cottage. But the cottages were all silent except for the sound of women weeping, because this was a night after a battle. Ay, they mourned for the men who had not returned to their homes.

"It was very hot, and after a while Saint Nicholas took Our Lady to a wood where a stream ran. Our Lady knelt down and drank a little of the water. She had no ornament on her head, so she could do that.

"When she left the silent land of the Cossacks, and went back to the sky, Saint Nicholas bade her farewell, because she had no more need of his guiding. Then he noticed that Our Lady's head was covered with a shining *kokoshynk*—a headdress of many, many pearls sewn together.

" 'Why,' he said, 'you have found a beautiful kokoshynk in the Cossack land.'

" 'No,' said Our Lady, 'I found them one by one.

*A rider tossed a pole with a horsetail over the wall.*

They are tears,' she said, 'of the Cossack mothers, shed for their dead.' "

The solitary old woman nodded, thinking of the legend. "And that is why to this day pearls are called tears in the Cossack land."

## XIX

## BATTLE AT SIMBIRSK

Perhaps the old Cossack woman had foreseen what would happen. But more likely she suspected that the Chief of the Cossacks would have to fight a pitched battle, and this proved to be the case.

There was a strong town on his way up the narrowing Volga. This was called Simbirsk. It had straggling

153

trading and farming settlements all around it. But on its high, terraced hill stood its castle wall. At Stenka Razin's approach the people of the outer town hurried forth to greet him.

The governor of Simbirsk, however, retired to the strong stone citadel on the hill. With him he took all the nobles and Muscovites and the four regiments of the garrison. He was Prince Miloslavsky, and he resolved to hold out on his hill.

Before doing anything, Stenka Razin surveyed the hill and the walls from all sides. He did not let his people charge recklessly against such a strong height. Instead, he ordered an earth rampart built around the bottom of the hill, and put all the cannon there to fire up at the castle. While that was being done, the experienced Cossacks pushed trenches up the hillsides and raised strong breastworks of heavy green logs just beneath the castle walls.

Then they attacked Prince Miloslavsky's citadel very much as if it had been a tall ship at sea. They hurled powder kegs over the walls to explode; they hoisted masses of burning hay on long poles to the top of the wall and tried to climb up beneath the smoke and flame.

The entire hill thundered by day with guns, and smoked with flames. Cheremiss and Mordva hunters shot burning arrows up into the air to fall on the roofs inside. Everywhere Stenka Razin directed the attack. The faithful Zamurza jumped before him to shield the Ataman with his own body. No bullet touched his master.

At night the Cossacks stole up with tree trunks which they raised silently against the wall, climbing swiftly and trying to seize the parapet.

Then the Tartars sounded their hand-drums and the Cossacks their bagpipes, and the fighting began again with the cry *"Sarin na kitchkou!"* Prince Miloslavsky became desperate and sent out messengers for help, but they were all captured. The Cossacks and their allies read the messages and believed that they would be masters of Simbirsk in a few more days.

The autumn frosts were beginning, and all around Simbirsk the forest turned scarlet and purple as if it, too, had taken part in the battle.

However, Stenka Razin knew that strong help was drawing near the besieged Muscovites. Tribesmen of the forest told him how a great army was marching in from Kazan at the last bend of the Volga.

What happened was that General Dolgoruki had mustered all the field troops of Moscow and sent them out to crush Stenka Razin's revolt. There were infantry regiments carrying new German firelock guns, and drilled by clever German officers; there were hussar regiments of horsemen—armed with breastplates and steel caps.

Both the Mordvas and Cheremiss people beset this army as it hurried through the forest. Yet the tribal hunters could do nothing much against disciplined, armored troops. And the best general of Moscow, Prince Iuri Boriatinsky, commanded this field army.

Unfortunately for him, Stenka Razin had not managed to capture Simbirsk before Prince Boriatinsky's army appeared. So the Chief of the Cossacks left his siege works to lead all his Cossacks and boatmen and tribal hunters against the advancing army.

Being between two enemies, he had to lead a swift attack on Boriatinsky's disciplined troops. The regiments from Moscow waited in solid ranks. They waited unyielding for their officers' command to fire on the charging masses of men.

Each time the Cossacks and the people rushed at the

line of troops, fire and shot blazed in their faces. If he had been on his fleet in the Volga, Stenka Razin would have won this last battle.

But on the land, his peasants, carrying only flails and spears and axes, melted into a confused mob at the volleys of the trained Muscovites. His Tartar horsemen could not stand their ground against the charge of the prince's armored hussars.

Only the Cossacks stood their ground. They held the center of the battlefield. Stenka Razin went from place to place among them, swinging his saber or flashing his pistols.

"Eh, brothers," he called to them. "The Cossacks still have powder. Their swords are still unbroken. Let us bite these dogs of Muscovites!"

Then he was wounded. At a charge of the iron hussars into the Cossack ranks, he stood against it until a saber cut deep into his skull. Then Zamurza lifted him up to his feet. After Zamurza was killed, a bullet tore through one of Stenka Razin's legs, and he could no longer stand.

These wounds caused him to lose the battle, because the ignorant peasants and rivermen thought that his magic had deserted him. After that some of them began to flee away in fright.

His Cossacks wanted him to retreat to the boats and seek refuge down the river. Stenka Razin would not do this. He knew how a war must be fought, and how little he could rely on the masses of people who followed him after his victories. It was clear to him that unless he won his way into Moscow itself, he could not win against the trained Muscovite troops.

So, although he suffered much from the wound in his head, and had to be carried about on a stretcher, he ordered the remainder of his army to hold fast to their siege earthworks, as the Don Cossacks had held their ramparts at Azov long before.

Now his Cossacks were besieged in their trenches. From the hill at Simbirsk and their camp at the forest edge, the Muscovites attacked the Cossack lines. So many were slain that the Cossacks barely had room enough to bury their dead. A single nun who had left her church to join them served as their only nurse.

Stenka Razin struggled against fever and weakness. When he became too ill to be carried about, the leaders of his Cossacks held a council to decide what to do.

*Then Stenka Razin was wounded.*

They decided to take him to the boats and embark themselves to escape down the Volga. By now Stenka Razin lay unconscious. More troops were marching in from Moscow, while the Cossacks were growing fewer each day.

When the Cossacks fled they left too few boats for the remaining peasants and rivermen. As soon as the steadfast Cossacks sailed away, the hussars of Prince

Boriatinsky charged against the mob of people and slaughtered them or drove them far into the timberlands.

No magic had ever protected the giant Ataman. It was simply his own will to stand against the power of Moscow that had all but conquered the great city. When he was seriously wounded he could no longer act as leader, even over his own Cossacks.

## XX

# THE HIDDEN COTTAGE

When the Cossacks took their wounded Ataman away down the river, he disappeared from the sight of the Muscovites. Snow began to cover the trails, and soon blizzards blinded travelers on the prairies. That winter the scouts from Moscow found out only that Stenka

Razin had been hidden somewhere in the steppes by his people.

Now the Muscovites knew that he was their most dangerous enemy. Besides protecting the escaped serfs, Stenka Razin stopped the hauling of ore from the mines of the Ural mountains, and prevented traffic from going up and down the Volga. By the reasoning of the Muscovites it was a crime for a Cossack to kill one of their Voevodes, while it was not wrong for a Voevode to kill a Cossack.

General Dolgoruki and his fellows knew their frontier would never be safe again as long as Stenka Razin lived. So they made haste to hunt him down, as hunters track down a wounded bear.

Through the winter storms they sent envoys to Cherkask, the headquarters of the Don Cossacks. There the old Ataman Yakublev had returned to power after the defeat of the Cossack Republic at Simbirsk. The aged man, who had never really believed Stenka Razin could win, made haste to pacify the officials from Moscow. He said the Cossacks of Cherkask had never revolted, that they had been loyal to the great Tsar.

"Then if you are indeed loyal subjects," said the

men from Moscow, "let every Cossack swear that he will obey only the Tsar henceforth."

This was more than Yakublev bargained for. By making excuses he put off swearing allegiance to Moscow. Some say the landowning Cossacks of Cherkask betrayed Stenka Razin. But it is more probable that the clever spies of Moscow got on the track of the wounded chief.

*His hiding place was deep in the steppes.*

He was not on the island of Kagalnik, which was al-most deserted by the people who had thronged to join the Cossack Republic. He was not at Samara or Sara-tov, where the people laid down their arms before the advancing Muscovite armies.

As soon as the snow melted and mud hardened in the roads, Prince Dolgoruki sent his armies questing toward the steppes. On every hand they met bitter re-sistance. The wild folk, the Chuvash and Mordvas, hid away in their forest retreats again. But peasants and hunters blocked the roads by felling trees across them; they attacked the army columns by driving frightened cattle before them. Sometimes they formed ranks to resist in the open, and terrible battles raged down the length of the frontier. All the steppe seemed to rise against the armies of Moscow.

The stern Dolgoruki terrorized towns on his way by penning captured rebels in the market squares and hanging their leaders at the gates. His road was marked by a trail of bodies.

Wherever the people heard a whisper that Stenka Razin might be on his way to join them, they fought against the Muscovite armies. But it was useless, with-out a leader.

What had happened was that Stenka Razin had been too badly wounded to ride out to them. He could only send messages that he would be with them soon.

His hiding place was deep in the steppes, on a small river. Perhaps he had gone back to his old home in the ravine where the cottage could not be seen from the plain.

There Alena tended his wounded head, and helped him walk out to three of the cherished horses he still kept with him. The faithful Filka came and went, bringing food and tidings of what was happening.

Stenka Razin made light of his misfortune. "Eh, little Alena," he would say, "it's this way with a Cossack. Sometimes he rides in joy, sometimes he walks in grief."

"And soon," she assured him, "you will be able to ride again."

The only joy the giant chief had was in her bright face. He knew that on the far Dnieper the Zaporog Cossacks were fighting battles of their own, and his people in Astrakhan were occupied with their fleet. They could not protect him. He could only limp out after daybreak to a tree where he watched his horses grazing on the rich grass.

The patrols of Prince Boriatinsky's army hunted the plain for a trace of Stenka Razin. They did not catch the wily Filka, but they soon discovered that fishermen knew where the Cossack chief had hidden. Then the Muscovites sighted the fine horses grazing above the ravine. Soldiers surrounded the cottage and stole up to the door.

The Cossacks say that Stenka Razin threw open the door and fought the Muscovites with his sword, driving them back until suddenly he stopped. Filka was not in the cottage, and Alena crouched weeping in the door. Stenka Razin looked around at the soldiers pressing toward him, and threw away his sword.

"Take me, dogs," he said to them. "I am ready."

Soon they caught Filka hurrying back to the cottage. Stenka Razin greeted his lieutenant with a jest. "Eh, Filka, now we'll ride into Moscow at last and all the Muscovites will throng to greet us."

That happened as he had said. But his captors were careful to make him appear like a condemned criminal. They seized the horses he loved. They took away his jeweled belt and sable cloak and fine silk shirt, dressing him in rags stinking of manure. They tied his arms to a post in the heavy cart, and chained Filka to the back of the cart.

Thousands of the Muscovites, beggars and painted noblewomen alike, lined the streets to the Red Place. They watched the cart trundling over the logs, bearing to his death the man they had been told was the chief of the Volga pirates.

First Stenka Razin was tortured by flogging and fire to make him cry out or beg for his life. He would not do that. Then he was taken out to the scaffold by the gate of the Kremlin. There waited the headsman of the Tsar, clad in dark red with his great ax.

In the throng that watched there were some Old Believers, peasants in sheepskins, silent bronzed Tartars. They say that Stenka Razin made no sound, and seemed to take no notice when he was bound fast to three heavy beams. The priest who had gone before him went away.

Then the bells of all the towers began to clash and ring in triumph.

The trumpets of the Kremlin guards sounded when the headsman swung his ax.

As to Filka, one story relates that after the death of

Stenka Razin, he seemed to be fearful—promising to lead his guards to the place where the Cossack chief had buried the treasure taken from Astrakhan. After that, Filka showed the Muscovites the way down to an island in the Don. There he pointed out a twisted willow tree. When his guards dug beneath the roots of the tree they found nothing.

Nor did they ever see Filka again. He had slipped into the swift gray water, and vanished.

## XXI

# LEGENDS OF THE STEPPES

All that summer of 1671 whirlwinds swept the steppes. Through the dust storms, blind bandura players felt their way from settlement to settlement of the Cossacks, to tell the people that Stenka Razin was lost.

They did this by chanting: *"Gone forever is Stenka Razin. Our brave chieftain they bound. They tied his kind hands. To Moscow the Mighty they bore him. And there on the wide Red Square—— They severed his stormy head."*

Through the steppes the message went: There was no longer a father of the homeless, a friend of the serfs, or a leader of all the Cossacks.

The people of the steppes and forest did not mourn. They were too accustomed to hardships on their frontier. For just a few years things had been good, under the Ataman of the Homeless; now bad times had come again.

But they did not forget Stenka Razin. The Cossacks of Astrakhan swept up the Volga again with the fleet of Vaska Usk. Astrakhan held out for a long time against the armies of the Tsar.

On the river Dnieper, the Zaporog Cossacks kept their freedom by fighting on their islands. On the Don the rich Cossacks of Cherkask had to submit finally, and swear that they would be subjects of Moscow.

Yet the monks of Solovetsky on the far White Sea defended their island monastery with cannon, like soldiers. They had to be conquered by a siege. And the Old Believers held to their faith elsewhere, migrating to the wilderness in bleak Siberia. Perhaps they were too ignorant to do otherwise, but they believed stubbornly that Christ had said that no one should be first and no one last among the people. So they would not humble themselves to others. Sometimes when families of the Old Believers were caught they crowded into their church and set fire to it, burning themselves to death rather than be driven from their home in the wilderness.

Even when a very strong Tsar came to the throne of Moscow, a generation after Stenka Razin, the miners of the Ural mountains and the Volga boatmen resisted his rule. This was the giant Tsar, called Peter the Great, who tried to do away with old customs and teach all the Russians the new ways he had learned in western Europe. At one time even the Streltsi turned against the inflexible Peter—until the foremost among them were tortured and put to death in the Red Place.

Peter ordered many new ships to be built on the Volga, to carry more trade up to inland Russia. It is often said that Peter was the father of the Russian navy; but as we have seen, Tsar Alexis, the son of Michael, tried to build the first fleet that Stenka Razin captured at Astrakhan.

As time went on, the Volga ceased to be the fron-

*All one summer they trekked east toward the rising sun.*

tier of the Muscovites. The river became the chief trade route of the Russian Empire, as it was now called. Just a century after Stenka Razin died, the descendants of the strange Kalmuks left their grazing lands on the river. They did not want to be herded into villages by the order of the Russian Tsars.

"You think you can go elsewhere," the governor from Moscow told the Khan of these Kalmuks, "but

you can't. You must abide here like a chained bear."

However, the Kalmuks had no intention of becoming chained. With all their families and herds they
journeyed away from their prairies between the Volga
and the Yaik. All one summer they trekked east toward
the rising sun until they were beyond reach of the
Russians.

After that the Russians did what they were rather

fond of doing—they changed the name of the river Yaik. They called it the Ural, and its frontier town of Yaisk, where Stenka Razin had found friends, became Uralsk, as it is called today.

About that time a clever German woman came to the throne of the Russian Empire—Catherine II, or Catherine the Great. And as late as Catherine's day, it seemed as if the ghost of Stenka Razin had come back to the Volga.

For a Cossack of the Don, named Pugachev, deserted from the army and took refuge in a monastery still kept by Old Believers. Then Pugachev rode out of the monastery to gather together the Cossacks along the Volga and the miners from the Ural—his object, to declare the serfs free and to lead his army up the river toward Moscow.

Again the Chuvash and Mordva hunters and the Cheremiss herdsmen joined this army of the Cossacks. Because everyone along the river remembered Stenka Razin so well, they almost believed that the daring Pugachev might be his spirit.

But Pugachev did not sail on the Volga fleet like Stenka Razin. After his capture his courage deserted him and he begged to be put to death without torture.

He did not have the strong spirit of the Ataman of the Homeless.

Even now in our time, the rivermen of the Volga, the Tartars of the prairies, the mountaineers of the mighty Caucasus and the Cossack families remember Stenka Razin.

If you ever go among these far-off people, and sit among them at the hour of evening quiet when the herds are driven home, and supper is eaten, and night birds take wing against the sunset, they will sing for you the song of Stenka Razin:

> *A falcon took flight*
> *Over the Volga.*
> *He looked not up at the skies,*
> *He stooped not to the lords below.*
> *Yet he sipped of the tawny water*
> *By the gates of Saratov,*
> *Of Tsaritzin, and Svialsk,*
> *And he asked of the river——*
> *Why are you sad, Mother Volga? . . .*

Yes, today the names of great lords like Iuri Boriatinsky and even the Tsar Alexis are all but forgotten. Yet this song of Stenka Razin is still sung, because there was no man like him on the river Volga in that distant day.

177

STENKA
RAZIN'S
COUNTRY

◆ Don Cossack forts and towns
♣ Muscovite frontier posts

BALTIC SEA

WHITE
SEA

MOSCOW

Dnieper R.

KRIM TARTARS

BLACK SEA

CONSTANTINOPLE

GREECE

TURKISH EMPIRE

MEDITERRANEAN SEA

# INDEX

181

# INDEX

# INDEX